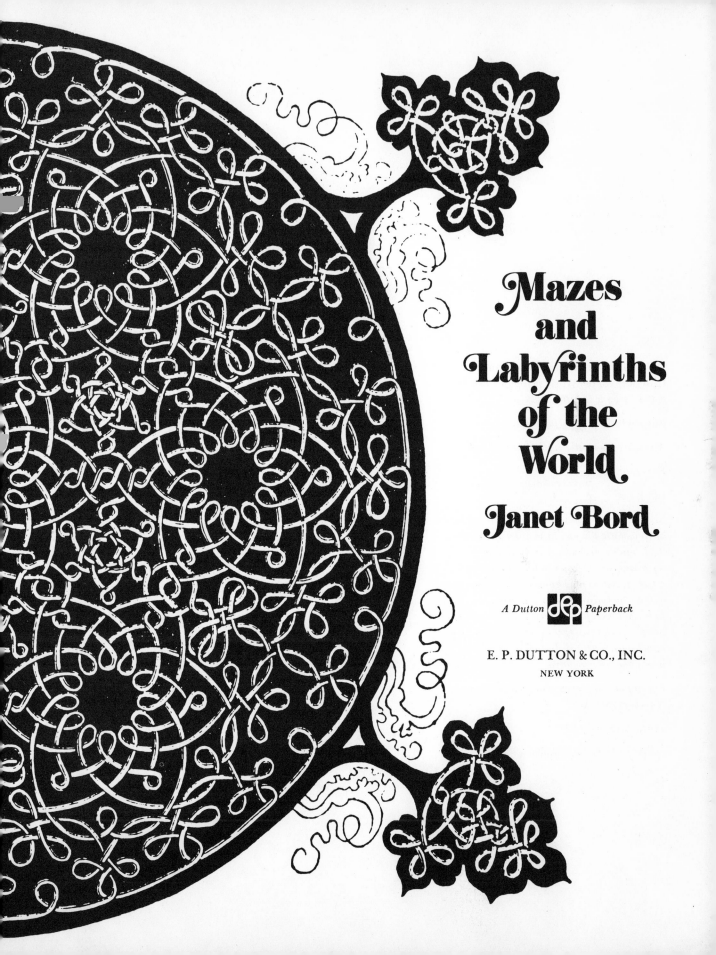

# Mazes and Labyrinths of the World

## Janet Bord

*A Dutton* **dep** *Paperback*

E. P. DUTTON & CO., INC.
NEW YORK

By the same author
Ghosts *(for children)*
Mysterious Britain *(with Colin Bord)*

*This paperback edition of* Mazes and Labyrinths of the World *first published by E.P. Dutton & Co., Inc. in 1976.*

*Copyright © 1975 by Janet Bord*

*First Edition*

*10   9   8   7   6   5   4   3   2   1*

*Library of Congress Catalog Card Number: 76-20262*

*ISBN: 0-525-47441-2*

*Designed by Gerald Cinamon*

# Contents

The world's a lab'rinth, whose enfractuous ways
    Are all compos'd of rubs and crook'd
                         meanders:
No resting here; he's hurry'd back that stays
    A thought; and he that goes unguided
                         wanders:
Her way is dark, her path untrod, unev'n;
    So hard's the way from earth, so hard's the
                         way to heav'n!

Francis Quarles,
*Emblems Divine and Moral,*
*Together With Hieroglyphics of the Life of Man*
(1777 edition)

## Mazes and Labyrinths

*'[The labyrinth] is ... at once the cosmos, the world, the individual life, the temple, the town, man, the womb – or intestines – of the Mother (earth), the convolutions of the brain, the consciousness, the heart, the pilgrimage, the journey, and the Way.'* – Jill Purce, *The Mystic Spiral*

Only two forms of the labyrinth or maze are widely known today – the hedge maze, and the maze as a children's puzzle. But these are two relatively recent developments of an image which has been in existence, and has had a special significance for people, for several thousand years. This book is an attempt to illustrate, in a pictorial way, how the labyrinth image has progressed from its earliest appearances in prehistoric rock carvings to its use in the twentieth century. This introduction is not intended as a history of mazes and labyrinths, for that task has already been comprehensively performed by W. H. Matthews in his book *Mazes and Labyrinths*. Instead, I shall introduce certain aspects of the theme which I myself find particularly intriguing, and which relate especially to its significance.

There are two main types of labyrinth: if the path from the outside to the centre has no false turnings, it is 'unicursal'; if there are dead ends, or a number of routes to the centre, then it is a 'multicursal' pattern. The names 'labyrinth' and 'maze' can be used interchangeably, though 'maze' suggests to me a multicursal design where confusion arises, and 'labyrinth' has become attached to the more ancient and symbolic forms.

The earliest labyrinth is usually thought to have been at Knossos on the island of Crete, where Theseus killed the Minotaur. Despite the familiarity of the Theseus story, and the fact that many people believe the labyrinth to have originated at Knossos, it may never have existed there as an actual construction. Some scholars have suggested that the name 'labyrinth' derives from *labrys*, double axe, and in fact means 'the place of double axes'. L. J. D. Richardson claims that the traditional Cretan labyrinth [50]* can be built up from a symbol which signified the double axe, thus lending more weight to this association of words.[1]

Sir Arthur Evans strongly discredited the idea that the Palace of Minos at Knossos was itself the labyrinth:

*The preconceived idea that the Palace that occupies the traditional seat of Minos was itself of a labyrinthine nature dies hard. In the days of ruin and desertion, with choked gangways and disordered lines of walling, with subterranean ducts, along which a stooping man might make his way, but which were really great stone-built drains, and, above all, the appearance of girl performers grappling with the charging bulls ... mysterious forms and features such as these, seen in the twilight of early saga, may well have called up the vision of the 'Greek Labyrinth' together with the monster that abode within its inmost lair.*[2]

Robert Graves suggested another possibility, that 'An open space in front of the Palace was occupied by a dance floor with a maze pattern used to guide performers of an erotic spring dance'.[3]

The first Cretan palaces were founded around 2000 B.C. But long before that time the idea of the labyrinth was known in Egypt. Around 3400 B.C. one of the earliest Egyptian tombs designed on the labyrinth principle had been constructed, that of King Perabsen of the Second Dynasty. Egyptian seals of later times (Sixth Dynasty, *c.* 2400–2300 B.C.) often bore more complex labyrinthine designs. The Labyrinth of Amenemhet III, a building of which few traces unfortunately now remain, is dated to the Eleventh Dynasty, *c.* 2000 B.C., and at that time there were close contacts between Crete and Egypt [38–44]. It might even be possible that Cretan architects and artists visited Egypt and learnt from their craftsmen. So it may be that the design of the Cretan labyrinth was influenced by Egyptian funerary practice. L. J. D. Richardson, however, suggests that the traditional 'Cretan labyrinth' design came about by accident, and he describes possible 'experimentation in arranging combinations of swastikas, meshed combs, meanders and the like' as envisaged by J. L. Heller.[4]

But the Mediterranean was not the only area where the labyrinth was known in pre-Christian times. Designs which are remarkably labyrinthine in appearance can be found carved on rock in several parts of northern Europe [15–22], and they are of early date. The recent

*The numbers in square brackets refer to the illustrations.

revolution in radio-carbon dating techniques[5] provides earlier dates than ever before for the long barrows, megaliths, camps and henges of Britain and north-west Europe, which are now thought to have been constructed between 4500 and 2500 B.C. The carvings just referred to presumably also date from this 2,000-year period. It seems likely therefore that the labyrinth pattern (in its broadest sense) was not in the first instance diffused outward from an original birthplace, but developed independently in more than one area. The significance it had was common to many peoples.

The most illuminating way of tracing the real origins of the labyrinth is to investigate its deeper significance. What did it mean to the peoples who actually used it, drawing it on the sand, carving it on the rock, cutting it in the turf? In the Seniang district of south-west Malekula, an island in the New Hebrides, a sand-tracing called 'The Path' [226] represented a design drawn in the sand by the female guardian ghost. The ghost of every dead man had to travel the same journey to the land of the dead, and this journey involved an encounter with the guardian ghost which is described here by A. Bernard Deacon:

*Ghosts of the dead . . . pass along a 'road' to Wies, the land of the dead. At a certain point on their way they come to a rock . . . lying in the sea . . . but formerly it stood upright. The land of the dead is situated vaguely in the wooded open ground behind this rock and is surrounded by a high fence. Always sitting by the rock is a female [guardian] ghost, [called] Temes Savsap, and on the ground in front of her is drawn the completed geometrical figure known as Nahal, 'The Path'. The path which the ghost must traverse lies between the two halves of the figure.*

*As each ghost comes along the road the guardian ghost hurriedly rubs out one half of the figure. The ghost now comes up, but loses his track and cannot find it. He wanders about searching for a way to get past the Temes of the rock, but in vain. Only a knowledge of the completed geometrical figure can release him from this impasse. If he knows this figure, he at once completes the half which Temes Savsap rubbed out; and passes down the track through the middle of the figure. If, however, he does not know the figure, the Temes, seeing he will never find the road, eats him, and he never reaches the abode of the dead.[6]*

If he successfully completed the partly-erased figure, the ghost could continue his journey to the land of the dead and be reborn into a new life. As with other sand labyrinths from the same part of the world [225, 227], this is

a labyrinthine figure to be got through, rather than a design with a circular form where the goal is at the centre, which is the form more frequently seen in the West.

The guardian ghost story links the labyrinth with death, and a successful negotiation of the pitfalls involved in setting out upon that inevitable journey. In its earliest use the labyrinth seems always to have been associated with death. The Cumaean gates at the entrance to Hades, guarded by a female sibyl (reminiscent of the Malekula guardian ghost), bore a representation of the Cretan labyrinth, according to the description in Virgil's *Aeneid*; labyrinthine carvings have been found on stones at the burial chamber of Bryn Celli Ddu on the island of Anglesey in Wales [17, 18]; some burial chambers in Ireland have stones carved with spirals, and those at Newgrange in County Meath [19, 20] are particularly impressive. Such spiral designs are probably forerunners of the true labyrinth; it certainly seems that they had the same significance. Karl Kerényi has shown[7] that both spirals and labyrinths were 'maps' of the underworld, and symbolic of death. The ingoing movement of the spiral indicates death, the outgoing rebirth. W. F. Jackson Knight links the two themes of death and rebirth with the labyrinth when he says that the labyrinth is a 'microcosm of the earth and a macrocosm of the human anatomy'.[8] In death one returns to the earth, the mother, from which one is eventually reborn. The presence of the labyrinth at burial structures signifies a ritual entry into the earth; the labyrinth represents both the earth and the human body as sources of life.

The body of the earth does in fact contain many spirals, according to research carried out by the late Guy Underwood. Working with his divining rod, he spent many years surveying ancient sites in Britain in order to plot the underground streams, and many times his results were in the form of spirals, as illustrated in his book *The Pattern of the Past*.[9] As we have just been linking the earth and the human anatomy, may these spirals perhaps echo the coiled entrails in the human body? (See also the passage on Babylonian entrail divination, on page 13.)

W. F. Jackson Knight expands his thoughts on death and rebirth in his book *Cumaean Gates*, where he suggests that some barrows 'were designed to represent the anatomy of a mother, in whom the dead might rest, in a pre-natal condition'. To many early peoples, all important phases of life had their special ceremonies of initiation, which were rebirth rituals. 'At each stage a man is reborn; and this applies to death. At death men are consigned to the earth, the universal mother from whom they came. They return to the earth, to be reborn.' This is the Greater Initiation; a Lesser Initiation can be achieved by following a maze or labyrinth to its heart. These two levels of initiation are clearly defined in the following quotation:

*While the Lesser Initiation was concerned with life and purgation from sin, the Greater Initiation was concerned with death and rebirth. For, as in the former the aspirant trod the winding paths of an intricate maze that signified our mortal life, and came at last through repentance to that clarity of intellect which is self-finding and self-mastery, so in the latter he was deemed to go through the grave itself, that thereby he might come face to face with the gods and learn the ultimate mysteries of existence.*[10]

Another aspect of the impenetrable labyrinth, as well as symbolizing a difficult route to be trodden before one's goal is reached, is the idea that the way through is known only to the initiate, and that unauthorized entry is therefore difficult. From this may have developed the use of the labyrinth as a symbol signifying 'no entry', for labyrinthine shapes were sometimes drawn on doorsteps to keep witches and evil spirits at bay. At one time this practice was widespread in Britain. In Scotland the traditional designs were traced in pipeclay on the thresholds and floors of byres, dairies and houses. The name for the designs was 'tangled threid', and their purpose appears in the verse

Tangled threid and rowan seed
Gar the witches lowse their speed.

Similar designs were also in use in the Hebrides, Isle of Lewis, Isle of Man, Wye Valley, Sussex and Wales, and in Knutsford in Cheshire it was traditional practice to trace a complicated design in sand on a bride's doorstep before she left home for her wedding. A quotation from John Layard[11] has a bearing on the latter example, showing how the earliest uses of the labyrinth were still perpetuated until recently, even though in a degenerate form. 'The object of the labyrinth was in the first place to exclude the uninitiated from participation in the life after death, and in the second *to exclude non-fertile or unlucky influences from the royal nuptials*' (my italics).

The same article by John Layard tells how the Dravidian populations of Southern India drew (the article was written in 1937, and I do not know if the practice still continues) designs on their thresholds during the unlucky Tamil month of Margali, mid-December to mid-January, when the sun dies after reaching the winter solstice. This month was unlucky because all kinds of epidemics were said to occur then. The designs were drawn only by the women, and were formed of any white powdery substance, such as slaked lime or old mortar ground fine. The lines were not preserved in any way once drawn; but the husband had to be the first to tread on them. The designs varied, but some were similar to the sand-drawings of the Malekula region, some were swastika-like, and some were the conventional Cretan labyrinth, which design they called 'the Fort'. Labyrinth tattoos were also known in the same part of India. In 1933 clay models of Greek houses were found near Corinth, which had meander patterns painted on their outer walls. W. F. Jackson Knight suggests[12] that these patterns had the same significance as the more recent 'tangled threid' – the exclusion of evil influences – and that both were 'devices of sympathetic apotropaic magic'.

A similar idea may also have been behind the design of the great earthwork called Maiden Castle, in Dorset, southern England [12]. The flat central area of 45 acres is surrounded by banks and ditches, and on the two shorter sides of its elongated area are entrances which employ a form of labyrinth to obstruct entry. This interpretation of the earthworks at Maiden Castle was first made by W. F. Jackson Knight in *Cumaean Gates*, and he succinctly describes such tactical labyrinths thus.

*The earliest tactical labyrinths are in some Egyptian forts of the First and Second Dynasties, about 3500 B.C. They have a system of walls with openings not opposite to each other but staggered, so that attackers have to take a long crooked path, moving laterally between the opening in one wall and the opening in the next. The plan enforces a labyrinthine path, and therefore achieves the correlative principles of conditional exclusion and conditional penetration. Friendly troops can freely use the path of entry; but an enemy, under enfilading fire for a long distance, is severely obstructed.*

Nevertheless, it has been estimated that it would require 250,000 men to defend this site, and it is therefore hard to believe that this construction was *originally* intended to be a defensive position. It may have been built for ritual purposes in the Neolithic era, when the labyrinthine entrances were used for processional entry, and in the Iron Age it became a fortress; so the labyrinthine entrances could have been useful in both peacetime and wartime. In peacetime, entry to the sacred site was allowed only to initiates, the restricted admission being symbolized by the labyrinthine entrances; and in wartime they were a useful defence feature, as already described.

Other ancient British earthworks are constructed of banks and ditches which in aerial photographs look vaguely suggestive of labyrinths, for example Badbury Rings in Dorset, and the Hereford Beacon. That these sites incorporated the labyrinth idea in their construction is merely speculation, but there is more evidence for the existence of some kind of three-dimensional labyrinth on Glastonbury Tor in Somerset [13]. It has been suggested that this was used for initiatory purposes:

*Candidates or pilgrims would have entered a three dimensional maze on the third path from the bottom and walked around the hill clockwise. Completing their first circuit they would have changed direction downwards, continuing anticlockwise for the second circuit and so on, contrariwise, for the seven full circuits of the maze . . . Candidates or pilgrims would have entered the paths in the order 3, 2, 1, 4, 7, 6, 5. The fifth path should sweep steeply to the summit but no clear evidence of its last stage is to be seen on the Tor today.*[13]

Glastonbury is not an unlikely site for a labyrinth, being linked with the stories of King Arthur, and the search for the Holy Grail which has been described as an initiation allegory.

To return to the theme of labyrinthine entrances used for defence, W. F. Jackson Knight also says in *Cumaean Gates* that the Chinese build 'spirit walls' at the entrances to their cities, set transversely to present a tortuous path which will deter evil influences from entering. House entrances are sometimes similarly constructed. 'If there are fine houses, they are concealed behind walls, and you cannot see into their courtyards through the gateways, because the gates are masked, on the inside, by another short section of wall, designed to prevent the ingress of evil spirits which (as everybody knows) can only fly in a straight line.'[14]

Treading a labyrinthine path, as in maze dances, may also have been used as an exclusion ritual, according to W. F. Jackson Knight. 'The movements of the performers are intended to weave a magical entanglement and spread a field of magical force to exclude all that is not wanted to enter the guarded place.'[15] The best-known maze dance is the Geranos (Crane) dance on the island of Delos, supposedly first danced by Theseus with the companions he had rescued from the clutches of the Minotaur in the Cretan labyrinth. Some of the participants wore animal masks, and the dance was performed round a horned altar, both of these being possible symbols of the bull-headed Minotaur. Another maze dance is still alive on Ceram, one of the Molucca Islands, and this commemorates the killing of Hainuwele the divine maiden. The ritual is described by Karl Kerényi as follows:

*Men and women linked alternately form a huge ninefold spiral. It is a* labyrinth, *the original model and later the copy of the labyrinth through which men have to pass when they die in order to reach the Queen of Hades and be ordained to human existence again. Hainuwele stands in the middle of the labyrinth, where a deep hole has been dug in the earth. In the slow convolutions of the spiral dance, the dancers press closer and closer towards her and finally push her into the pit. The loud three-voiced Maro chant drowns the maiden's cries. They heap earth upon her, and the dancers stamp down firmly over the pit with their dancing feet.*[16]

Maze dances have been (and still are, in some cases) practised in several Western countries, for example Italy, Corfu, Greyerz (Western Switzerland), Munich (the Schäffler dances performed every seven years), Traunstein in Upper Bavaria (Sword Dance, associated with St George and his dragon-killing feat which perhaps has echoes of Theseus killing the Minotaur). Ropes are featured in some of the dances, including the Crane Dance, and it has been suggested that these could represent the clue of thread which Theseus followed in his escape (or rebirth) from the labyrinth. (It has also been suggested that this thread in turn may represent the umbilical cord.) A rope also had a vital part to play in the story of the wooden horse which was pulled into Troy (this city was itself a kind of labyrinth, being difficult of entry), and the movements of the men who pulled the horse have been compared to the movements of the maze dancers. W. F. Jackson Knight links the story of the Trojan horse with mortuary myth – 'The entry into Troy is conceived as entry, at death or initiation, into the earth.'[17] He also feels that the horse itself may have echoes of the Minotaur. The image of the Trojan horse being pulled by a rope through the labyrinthine city of Troy, 'pregnant in its cavernous bowels with armed men',[18] is echoed in the following quotation:

*Meandering or labyrinthine paths, spirals, mazes, actually followed in ritual (initiation) dances, or symbolically represented in ritual objects, represent the archetypal endeavours of the divine ancestor, the prototypical man, to emerge into this world, to be born. In the ceremony of the Dog totem in Northern Australia, 'a winding path is cut through the bush for a processional march, which represents at the same time the flounderings of the ancestral beast through the primeval mud, and also the rope by which it was drawn onto dry land by the human companion.'* This is what Freud meant by anal birth: *'I cannot help mentioning how often mythological themes find their explanation through dream interpretation. The story of the Labyrinth, for example, is found to be a representation of anal birth; the tortuous paths are the bowels, and the thread of Ariadne is the umbilical cord.'*[19]

Religious rituals degenerate over the centuries until the remaining movements bear little resemblance to the original, and the meaning is hard to discern. Such dances as the Crane Dance just described may also have been performed in the mazes and labyrinths still to be found in other parts of the world, for example the stone mazes of Scandinavia and the turf mazes of England. Although no rituals are performed on the turf mazes today, nor have been for several hundred years (a sad fact which is best illustrated in Shakespeare's words in *A Midsummer Night's Dream* – 'The nine men's morris is fill'd up with mud; And the quaint mazes in the wanton green, For lack of tread, are undistinguishable:'), there are records of them having been used on such festive occasions as Easter. This was a time for celebration of the resurrection, and the incorporation of maze-running games and dances would be particularly appropriate in view of the symbol's connection with rebirth. Maze-running probably also featured in May Day festivities, when the reawakened fertility of the earth, and of mankind, after a long winter were celebrated. Other traditional ceremonies of May-time, including Morris dancing and hobby horse festivals, may also be connected with the ancient significance of the labyrinth, and this possibility is discussed later [91, 92].

It is recorded that Swedish peasants living in Finland used to use the stone mazes in that country for running games in which the young men would run through them to a girl at the centre; other accounts mention a stone coffer grave at the centre, another link between the maze and death. No doubt running games of this kind were played throughout Scandinavia (stone mazes have also been found in Norway, Sweden and Denmark), not just in Finland.

There seems to be no clear evidence as to the time when the stone and turf mazes were first built and cut. In name they are often linked with Troy (names like Troy Town, Walls of Troy, Tröjeborg are frequently seen), and it has been supposed that they were named

after the famous city. But W. F. Jackson Knight suggests (and he is not alone in this belief) that 'Troy' *describes* a maze or labyrinth. 'Troy', 'Troja', 'Troia' and other variations may be derived from the Celtic root *tro*, meaning 'to turn', and expressing the idea of a rapid revolution such as would occur in a ritual dance through the maze. (The Welsh *troi* means 'to turn, to revolve'.) Knight concludes:

*The safest thing to do is to suppose that Homer's Troy and all the other Troys were called after the word used for mazes and labyrinths. Troy was called Troy because it had some quality of a maze. The obvious definition of this quality is as follows. A maze is a material or magical instrument of shutting, and Troy was very much a shut city.*[20]

Another sidelight on this question of 'Troy' was mentioned in *Cumaean Gates*, when Knight described some Babylonian tablets [8] dated to around 1000 B.C. These are marked with spiral forms said to represent animal intestines, and the tablets were used for entrail divination. One of them was inscribed *ékal tiráni* – 'palace of the intestines' – and Knight tells us that the name 'Troy' has been compared to the word *tiráni*, intestines.[21]

The 'bower' or 'bore' part of names like Julian's Bower and Gilling Bore may be derived from the Anglo-Saxon *burg* or *burh*, 'city', allied to *beorgan*, 'to protect'. This leads us to another suggested interpretation: that turf or stone mazes were originally made to protect places of importance in their immediate vicinities, rather in the nature of the threshold designs described earlier. Several of the still existing turf mazes are near to sites of known antiquity: the maze on St Catherine's Hill, Winchester, is within an Iron Age camp; Breamore maze, Hampshire, is on a hill covered with Celtic fields, and close to a long barrow (it is also remote from the mediaeval and modern villages, and the location is a strange one if it was constructed purely for festive purposes); the maze at Wing in Rutland is close to a large tumulus. So despite the beliefs of certain scholars that the traditional mazes of Northern Europe are relatively recent in origin, possibly being derived from the designs still to be found in some European churches, there is reason to believe that there were mazes in stone and turf long before the mediaeval church builders began incorporating them in their designs. The church mazes may have been copies of the stone and turf mazes; or perhaps the stone and turf mazes were recut to resemble the church mazes when a Christian interpretation began to be placed on them.

Church mazes, often of tiles but sometimes carved in stone, are rare in Britain but well distributed in Europe, especially in France and Italy, though many have been destroyed. The traditional religious interpretation is that they were constructed to represent the folds of sin which bar man's pilgrimage to Heaven. They were sometimes called 'Chemin de Jérusalem', and following a maze was a substitute for a pilgrimage to the Holy Land. The pilgrims sometimes traversed them on their knees, as a penance. But they may have had a less down-to-earth significance to their builders, a significance again linked to the use of the labyrinth symbol as a protection against evil: they could have been constructed to protect both the church and the worshipper from evil influences, the worshipper gaining added protection by ritually following the course of the maze to its heart.

The labyrinth means different things to different people, and its continued popularity through the ages obviously indicates its importance. Having immersed myself in labyrinths, I do not find this hard to accept. The designs have a powerful effect – but in a beneficial way, in that a strong awareness of them provides a soothing influence. I think this must be because as symbols they are complete and balanced, and therefore satisfying.

I do not claim that my collection of pictures is exhaustive. It would be a life's work to try and search out every example; and it would be a search without end, because the labyrinth symbol is still in frequent use, as the final pages of the book show. The pictures are placed in a rough chronological order, in an attempt to show how the original symbol has been developed or refined according to the meaning it had for later peoples and the uses to which it has been put.

### Related Symbols and Sites

[1] Before introducing the earliest-known true labyrinths, it is relevant to take a look at some associated symbols which have been used by artists in past centuries in various parts of the world. The swastika is a very ancient symbol found in many primitive societies; and the interpretations given to it are as varied as its distribution is widespread. When it is elaborated with 'meanders', as on this drawing of a ram from an archaic Greek vase, it has many similarities to some square labyrinths. This vase also shows a band in a meander design, a pattern which also seems to echo the labyrinth.

[2] The designs on this Bronze Age cinerary urn found at San Marino, near Albano, Italy, include swastikas enclosed in panels which themselves suggest labyrinths. (The panels also suggest the plan for the game of nine men's morris [93].) Around the neck is another labyrinthine design. As the labyrinth is associated with death, it is not surprising to see designs like this on a burial urn; and the pots themselves were often symbolic of the body and womb of the mother.

[3] Swastikas can be found in the most unlikely places. This row of them was carved by the twelfth-century south doorway of Great Canfield church, Essex. Were they perhaps carved here as a protection symbol?

(This photograph presents an optical illusion, probably due to the lighting at the time the photograph was taken. The paler lines, which are in fact the carved strokes, may appear to be raised, and thus the swastikas will be diffi-cult to see. Then suddenly the lines will change their appearance, and the swastikas become clear.)

[4] It has been suggested that Celtic inter-lace designs are plans of winding maze dances. This Celtic cross at Carew, Pembrokeshire, has several swastikas at the top, as well as the interlaced designs at the bottom.

[5] This ornate relic, the shrine of St Patrick's bell (dating from A.D. 1091–1105), is decorated with elaborately interwoven designs which may origin-ally have had the same symbolic signi-ficance as spirals and labyrinths.

[6] Another example of an object which has associations with death and which is decorated with symbols of a labyrinthine type is this Chinese bronze ritual vessel of the type *chüeh*. At the time of the Shang Dynasty (*c.* 1500–1027 B.C.) vessels such as this were used for pouring libations of wine to the spirits, and were buried in royal and other tombs. The maze-like symbol is usually described by scholars as a thunder pattern, this name deriving from the similarity of the ancient form of the Chinese character for thunder and the shape of the individual design units.

[7] Spirals can be thought of as elementary unicursal labyrinths, for they have an indirect path leading to a hidden centre. It is interesting how similar is the design on this drawing of an ancient bronze agafe or belt plate from Koban, in the Caucasus (U.S.S.R.) to the linked spirals carved on one of the stones inside the Newgrange tumulus [19].

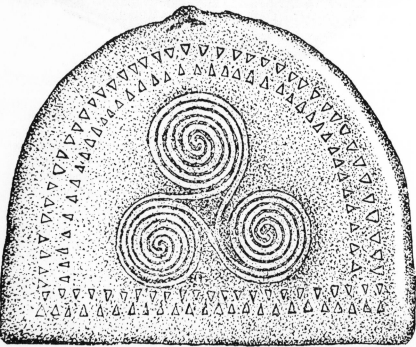

[10, 11] Geoffrey Russell has suggested[22] that the heart of the traditional Cretan labyrinth bears a strong resemblance to the early Christian symbol, the Chi-Rho. This monogram is a combination of the two Greek letters X and P, which begin the name of Christ (ΧΡΙΣΤΟΣ), and it originated in a dream which the Emperor Constantine had on the eve of a battle in A.D. 312. He was 'admonished in a dream to paint on his soldiers' shields the heavenly sign of God, and so to give battle. He does as he is commanded, and with the letter X placed transversely, having one extremity bent round, he marks their shields with Christ'.[23]

There are several variations of the Chi-Rho, but that shown here (*left*), with the P open, most closely echoes the

[8] Babylonian tablets used for entrail divination and dated to around 1000 B.C. are marked with spiral forms which represent animal intestines.

[9] An elementary labyrinth can be seen in the lower part of a broken figurine of the Vinča civilization (*c.* 5300–3500 B.C.) from Yugoslavia. This artefact was found at Agino Brdo near Belgrade.

centre of the labyrinth, and also the description in Constantine's dream – 'having one extremity bent round.' Also illustrated is a Cretan labyrinth for comparison. The Chi-Rho monogram is on a stone at Kirkmadrine, Wigtownshire, Scotland; the labyrinth is on a coin of Knossos, dating from the first or second century B.C. (shown upside-down for ease of comparison).

Geoffrey Russell likens the Chi-Rho in the labyrinth to Christ the Good Shepherd's crook, and comments, 'Perhaps the loop of the crook was closed, as a refinement, to indicate that the [labyrinth] game had been played for the last time and the spirit was safely enclosed with the Saviour.'

[12, 13] Two hills in southern England
may incorporate labyrinths – Maiden
Castle in Dorset (*below*) and Glastonbury Tor in Somerset (*right*). The
former may have been a tactical labyrinth
to obstruct entry, the latter an initiatory labyrinth. Both sites are described
more fully in the introduction.

[14] Two architectural mazes have been discovered this century on the Greek mainland, one at the site of the Oracle of the Dead in the province of Epirus, and the other (illustrated here) at Epidaurus, where the sanctuary of Asclepius, god of healing, was located. The tholos (circular building) at Epidaurus adjoined the temple of Asclepius, and its purpose is still unknown. It has been interpreted as the tomb of the god, where patients came searching for a cure; or as a pit for Asclepius's sacred snakes. The building consisted of six concentric circles, the outer three supporting its outer columns (Doric), wall, and inner colonnade (Corinthian), while the inner three formed a kind of miniature labyrinth.

## Ancient Labyrinthine Carvings

[15] Enigmatic rock carvings given the name of 'cup and ring marks' are found largely in the north of England and Scotland, but are not unknown elsewhere. Their purpose is unclear, despite a multitude of theories which have been put forward, one of which sees them as rudimentary labyrinths. There are several different styles, some of them illustrated on this drawing of cup and ring marks (*above right*) at Auchnabreach, in Argyllshire, Scotland. Note that the three linked spirals are in evidence again.

[16] Cup and ring marks probably date from the Neolithic period, as do the megalithic tombs illustrated in this part of the book. These examples (*opposite*) can be seen carved on a rock face at Roughting Linn, Northumberland. Carvings resembling cup and ring marks and elementary labyrinths can also be found in other parts of Europe, and the rock engravings at Bohuslän, Sweden, are particularly striking.

[17, 18] The passage grave of Bryn Celli Ddu on the island of Anglesey, Wales, illustrates very clearly the link between labyrinthine forms and death. First the plan of the cairn itself suggests a maze; second, a small broken spiral design was found on a standing stone; and third, a more elaborate, wandering design can be seen on a stone which now stands upright where the centre of the mound would have been. In the original excavation this stone was found lying over a pit containing burnt bones. This decorated stone can be seen in the photograph, and the accompanying drawing shows the design more clearly. The lower part of the drawing carries the design seen in the photograph; and the central band and upper part illustrate the designs on the narrow upper edge and the other face of the stone respectively.

W. F. Jackson Knight comments: 'The spirals in this monument invite the explanation that they were all intended, with more or less clearness of purpose, to shut or seal the burial, or at least to suggest or assist that requirement. The spiral plan can hardly mean anything else, with its long and bewildering path. The stone with the leaf-shaped, zigzag, maze-like pattern may have been set up during burial rites, either as a chart to direct dancing, or as a symbol of exclusion from the land of the dead, and correlative admission to it; no doubt it was carefully buried inside the monument in order to maintain a similar effect by its sympathetic presence.'[24]

[19, 20] The passage grave at Newgrange in County Meath, Ireland, is one of the finest prehistoric monuments in that part of the world. The mound is 45 feet high and 265 feet across, and the internal chamber is 20 feet high. Some of the stones at Newgrange are richly decorated with spiral designs, especially the entrance stone (*right*). Illustration 19 shows the interior of the burial chamber. Once a year, on the morning of the winter solstice, the sun shines right inside the chamber through a specially contrived slit in the roof, and illuminates the three linked spirals.

[21] The latest radio-carbon dating methods give a date of around 3500–3000 B.C. for the megalithic chambered tombs of North-West Europe. Another example containing elaborately carved stones is illustrated in this drawing of the interior of a tumulus at Slieve-na-Calliagh in County Meath, Ireland.

[22] The half-circle design seen in the previous illustration also appears on stones in the gallery grave of Gavr'Innis island in Brittany (Department of Morbihan), North-West France.

[23] Ancient rock engravings in other parts of Europe sometimes include labyrinthine designs. The designs shown here are very similar to the cup and ring marks previously illustrated. They were found in Spain at Mogor, near Marin, Pontevedra Province.

[24] Also found at Mogor was this carving of a labyrinth of the traditional Cretan design. Such examples as this are notoriously difficult to date, but the obvious Cretan influence would suggest that it is just over 2,000 years old.

[25–28] An important group of rock carvings has been discovered in the Camonica Valley in the Italian Alps north-east of Milan. The oldest carvings date from the Neolithic period, and the changes in style show that carving was continued up to the Roman Conquest. Labyrinth designs occur frequently. Some incorporate figures or faces at the centre, or just two dots to

represent eyes – perhaps showing a monster as an integral part of the labyrinth. Later designs show Greek influence, and the Cretan-style labyrinth shown here is dated to around 300 B.C. The others are roughly dated to the third or second millennia B.C.

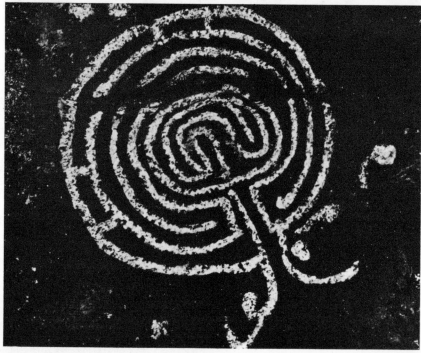

[29–31] Another rock engraving from the Camonica Valley shows an animal whose tail becomes a labyrinth [30]. This is similar to a carving on a mediaeval tomb (called the Pegasus Stone) among the Bogomil graves at Mesići in Bosnia,

29

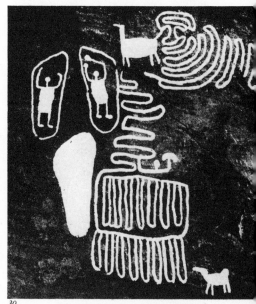

30

Yugoslavia, where an animal has a labyrinth as a tail [29]. Illustration 31 is a drawing of the maze on the winejar from Tragliatella [90]. Here too the maze forms the horse's tail.

31

[32] The labyrinth is commonly associated with the area of the Mediterranean centred on Crete and perhaps the earliest extant representation of what has become accepted as the traditional Cretan design was discovered recently at Pylos, near Navarino in Southern Greece. A clay tablet dated to *c.* 1200 B.C. bears a labyrinth design drawn when the clay was soft. It has been described as a 'doodle', perhaps similar in intention to another labyrinth design found scored on a tile from the Acropolis at Athens. The exposed surface of the tile bore an elaborate design, but the hidden surface, revealed when the tile fell from its place on the crested ridge of a pediment, showed a labyrinth design. It has been suggested that it was a craftsman's secret mark.

[33] The conventional Cretan labyrinth design has been diffused to many distant lands, as the illustrations hereabouts show. One example not too far removed from Crete was found traced on a pillar in the House of Lucretius, Pompeii, in Italy. Pompeii was engulfed following the eruption of the volcano Vesuvius in A.D. 79, so this graffito must be around 2,000 years old. The inscription reads LABYRINTHUS HIC HABITAT MINOTAURUS, which Trollope suggests was intended to mean 'Here lives a great beast'![25]

[34] Britain also has carvings showing the traditional Cretan-type labyrinth. This is one of two small carvings which were discovered as recently as 1948, side by side on a vertical rock face beneath undergrowth on the slopes of a gorge known as Rocky Valley, near Tintagel, Cornwall.

[35] A carving of a similar design to those in Rocky Valley was discovered in 1908 on a stone by the side of a track in the Wicklow Mountains of Ireland. The stone is 3 feet 9 inches high and has become known as the Hollywood Stone because it was found near Hollywood in the townland of Lockstown. The lane where it was found is only a couple of hundred yards from the road leading to Glendalough, at one time an important religious centre, and this has led to the suggestion that the carved stone was a religious way-marker. Another idea is that this maze and those at Rocky Valley (plus, perhaps, others not yet discovered) may have been 'visiting cards' left by travelling craftsmen who were of Minoan or Mycenaean origin. The Hollywood Stone is now in the National Museum of Ireland, and in 1964–65 it was exhibited at the World's Fair in New York, where it attracted much attention.

[36] This 'maze stone' is in a small park 5 miles west of Helmet, California, U.S.A. It has been given the (unbelievable) dating of 13,000 B.C., and has been ascribed to the Cascadians, ancestors of the Maya. Others suggest it is of Buddhist origin, five Buddhist missionaries having sailed over 7,000 miles in a junk from the Orient to California in A.D. 458. (At least this date is more reasonable.) Such a journey may not have been impossible, because it was reported that during the years from 1782 to 1875, more than forty junks had drifted to the west coast of North America.

[37] The influence of the traditional Cretan design can again be seen, this time in a labyrinth carved on stone at Oraibi in Arizona, U.S.A., 90 miles east of the Grand Canyon. Both circular and square labyrinths feature in the culture of the Hopi Indians, other examples being found at the Casa Grande ruins in the Gila valley of Southern Arizona, and on a rock near the Hopi pueblo of Shipaulovi in Northern Arizona. The design has also been incorporated into North American Indian craftwork [241, 242].

It has been suggested that the labyrinth may have been introduced from Europe as late as the mid seventeenth century A.D., when the Hopi had many European contacts. For example, a Franciscan Mission was established less than 2 miles from Shipaulovi in 1629. However, it has also been suggested that the labyrinth was the Mother Earth symbol to the Hopi, representing spiritual rebirth, and the beliefs relating to this, described in *Book of the Hopi* by Frank Waters,[26] are very similar to those from other parts of the world.

**Egyptian Tombs, Temples and Seals**

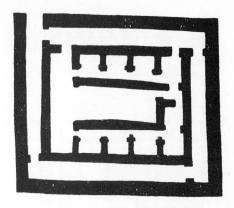

[38] The construction of early Egyptian tombs seems to suggest an elementary labyrinth. An example is the tomb of King Perabsen of the Second Dynasty (*c.* 3400 B.C.), a plan of which is shown here. The tomb was in the central chamber, which was surrounded by a passageway with projecting masonry at intervals, probably indicating where doors originally barred the way. This tomb marked the beginning of a new style in tomb construction, apparently with concealment or exclusion as the aim. Only those duly qualified might enter the royal tombs. Later, mortuary temples were built outside the tombs, and the labyrinth form was transferred from tomb to temple, where the funerary rites of the dead king-god were performed.

[39–41] The temple of Amenemhet III, built beside his pyramid in Fayoum, was described as 'the Labyrinth of Egypt' by Herodotus, Strabo, Diodorus the Sicilian, Pliny and others. Part of Pliny's description reads: 'There is no doubt that Daedalus took from this the pattern of his labyrinth, which he made in Crete. Although he only copied the hundredth part of it, since it contained winding ways and bewildering twists and turns . . . with many entrances designed to produce misleading goings and comings . . . Those who go through its laborious windings with their baffling intricacy, come by slopes to lofty chambers . . . Some of the temples are so devised that those who approach the doors are greeted by terrific thunders from within. The passages are for the most part in darkness.'

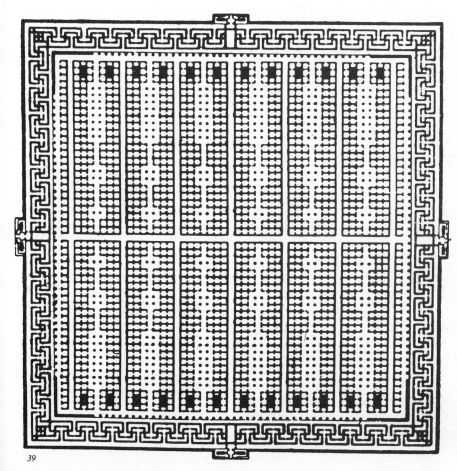

39

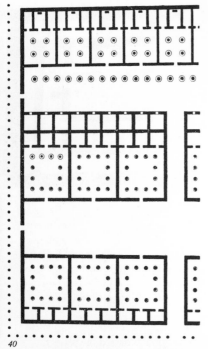

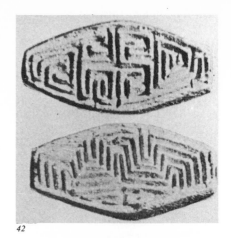

The Labyrinth, constructed around 2000 B.C., was destroyed in Roman times and a town built on the site. It was not until 1888 that the exact location of the Labyrinth was established, by Professor Flinders Petrie. The illustrations show plans of two suggested restorations, one by the Italian archaeologist Canina [39] and one by Professor Petrie [40] (showing the western half only). Illustration 41 shows one of the small pieces of sculpture retrieved from the site. The king, kneeling in a boat, is opening the door of a shrine containing a sacred tree.

[42–44] Labyrinthine patterns also appear on Egyptian seals and plaques. The patterns on the seals have been found impressed on the fastenings of jars in royal tombs, again providing a definite link between the labyrinth and death. Illustration 42 shows two seals of the

40

42

43

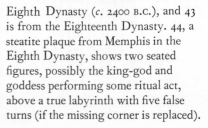

Eighth Dynasty (*c.* 2400 B.C.), and 43 is from the Eighteenth Dynasty. 44, a steatite plaque from Memphis in the Eighth Dynasty, shows two seated figures, possibly the king-god and goddess performing some ritual act, above a true labyrinth with five false turns (if the missing corner is replaced).

41

## The Cretan Labyrinth

[45, 46] The location of the original Cretan labyrinth has never been definitely established. Some writers of antiquity decided that the legend began in one of the complexes of caves and quarries on the island, possibly that near Gortyna in the south, where the passages are truly labyrinthine. The French botanist G. P. de Tournefort explored the Gortyna caves in 1700: 'This famous place is a subterranean Passage in manner of a Street, which by a thousand Intricacies and Windings, as it were by mere Chance, and without the least Regularity, pervades the whole Cavity or Inside of a little Hill at the foot of Mount Ida . . . The Entrance into this Labyrinth is by a natural Opening, seven or eight Paces broad, but so low that even a middle-siz'd Man can't pass through without stooping.'

C. R. Cockerell explored the cavern at the beginning of the nineteenth century, and his party wisely took a length of string with them. He comments: 'The clearly intentional intricacy and apparently endless number of galleries impressed me with a sense of horror and fascination I cannot describe. At every ten steps one was arrested, and had to turn to right or left, sometimes to choose one of three or four roads. What if one should lose the clue!'

The engravings show the entrance to one of the caves (*above*), and a plan of the passages (*right*). It is probably the cavern near Gortyna, which was the best known.

The identification of a labyrinth with a cave is not impossible. Caves had a great attraction for early man, and he often chose, for the performance of his rituals, caves difficult of access. The cave may have represented for him the link between his world and the world of the dead, the way into the body of the Earth Mother. It seems likely that megalithic tombs were derived from cave burials – the tombs represent artificial caves, with the corpse curled up in a foetal position inside the womb of the Earth Mother.

One link between labyrinths and caves comes in the word 'labyrinth' itself, which is thought to mean 'place of stone'. What better 'place of stone' than a cave?

W. F. Jackson Knight's words sum up the close association between caves and labyrinths: 'The labyrinth is a boundary between without and within; it is the entrance to the tomb, it is the cave which is the entrance to the earth, and possibly it is the body of the earth mother, and of the divine king also.'[27]

*47*

*48*

*49*

*50*

*51*

*52*

[47–52] The Cretan labyrinth has been depicted on the coins of Knossos, sometimes in square form, sometimes rounded [11], and sometimes merely suggested by meander patterns. A meander round the figures of divine and royal persons was symbolic of protection; the bull was an emblem of divinity; in Egypt, a star or rosette was an emblem of royalty.

The six coins here are dated as follows: 47 from 500–430 B.C., 48 and 49 from 430–350 B.C., 50 is probably from the second century B.C., 51 is from the second or first centuries B.C., and 52 is from the first century B.C.

[53] The legendary history of the Cretan labyrinth tells that it was built by Daedalus on the instructions of Minos, King of Crete (who later became a judge in Hades, the underworld – is this purely a coincidental link between the labyrinth and death?). The labyrinth housed the Minotaur, half bull, half man, who was the offspring of Minos's wife Pasiphaë and a bull. The Athenians, as a result of some past adventure, were bound to send Minos seven young boys and seven maidens every ninth year (though not all authorities agree on this number of years; see, for example, J. G. Frazer below), and these were offered to the Minotaur. Theseus, the great Athenian hero, may have been among the tribute on one occasion. Be that as it may, he resolved to kill the Minotaur, for if that could be done the tribute would in future be cancelled.

Minos's daughter Ariadne was attracted by Theseus, and wishing to help him she took the advice of Daedalus and gave him a clue of thread by which he could retrace his steps and escape from the labyrinth. Reaching the centre, he killed the Minotaur and leaving the labyrinth with the boys and girls intended for sacrifice, they all set sail for home. En route, they landed on Delos, where they celebrated their victory with the Crane Dance.

J. G. Frazer's interpretation of the Minotaur story, given in *The Golden Bough*,[28] is an interesting one rarely aired. He details his theory, and concludes: 'On the whole the foregoing evidence ... points to the conclusion that at Cnossus the king represented the sungod, and that every eight years his divine powers were renewed at a great festival, which comprised, first, the sacrifice of human victims by fire to a bull-headed image of the sun, and, second, the marriage of the king disguised as a bull to the queen disguised as a cow, the two personating respectively the sun and the moon.'

Theseus's defeat of the Minotaur has frequently been depicted by artists. The photograph shows a kylix or bowl from Vulci, Etruria, which illustrates Theseus's major exploits, the centre panel being reserved for his victory over the Minotaur. The meander patterns are probably intended to represent the labyrinth.

[54] Ariadne's clue of thread is depicted as a spiral on this terracotta relief (on an ornament belonging to a large vase in Corneto Museum). The thread seems to come from her head, and this is reminiscent of the 'silver cord' which sometimes features in cases of astral projection, when a person's astral body separates from the physical body. Sometimes (but not invariably) the two bodies are seen to be joined by a cord, and they are usually joined at the head. It is said that at death the cord is broken and the astral body leaves the physical for ever. This idea bears thinking about, in view of the links between the spiral and the labyrinth and death.

[55] The slaying of the Minotaur is only one feature of this panoramic painting, entitled 'Theseus and Ariadne'. Dating from the fifteenth century, it

is from the Italian School. In this
and all other depictions of the
Cretan labyrinth, it is shown as a
unicursal design, and one would think
that Ariadne's clue of thread was
therefore superfluous. The only occasion
on which it would be useful would
be if the passages of the labyrinth were
dark. If Theseus had stopped and
turned round for some reason, he might
have forgotten which way he was facing!

[56] Another Italian depiction of Theseus
and the labyrinth comes from the
Florentine Picture Chronicle. This early
drawing is attributed to Baccio Baldini.

[57] This engraving, of the school of Finiguerra, may have been based on the drawing from the Florentine Picture Chronicle. The clue of thread can be seen securely fixed to a hook at the entrance to the labyrinth.

[58] Volume 8 of Ovid's *Metamorphoses* is the source of this engraving of Theseus. The lady must be Ariadne, for she holds a string presumably intended as the 'clue of thread'.

[59] The killing of the Minotaur in the earlier illustrations seems somehow unreal and purely symbolic; this more recent representation of the legend, by Thomas Erat Harrison, a Victorian sculptor, painter and etcher, is stark and there is no doubt that Theseus has no pity for the subjugated Minotaur. This picture is also interesting for its unusual interpretation of the labyrinth, which is presumably the winding roads, steps and bridges round the peaks on the left.

[60] This seventeenth-century engraving by Johann Wilhelm Baur illustrates another aspect of Theseus's story. After he had killed the Minotaur, he abandoned Ariadne on Delos, where she was rescued by the god Dionysus (or Bacchus – god of wine and ecstatic liberation). He married her; and after her death he placed her wedding garland in the sky as a constellation, the Corona Borealis.

[61] Daedalus helped Ariadne to rescue Theseus from the labyrinth by making the clue of thread for her to give him. When King Minos learned of this, he imprisoned Daedalus in the labyrinth with his son Icarus. The ingenious Daedalus made wings from wax and feathers, and he and Icarus flew away. Despite his father's warnings, Icarus flew too high and the sun melted the wax, causing him to plummet into the sea. The tragedy is shown in this bas-relief (measuring 4 feet 10 inches by 2 feet 9 inches) on a wall in the courtyard of the Hôtel du Grand Maître de France, in Compiègne, France.

[62] This curious representation of Theseus killing the Minotaur (and Icarus falling from the sky) is dated 1673. It appears to be an advertisement for a firework display called 'Irrgarten Daedali' (Labyrinth of Daedalus) to be held in Vienna. The engraving is by Johann Jacob Köchly and Johann Martin Lerch.

[63, 64] A labyrinth with the Minotaur at its centre was often used as an emblem. This sixteenth-century seal [63] bears the same design as one shown in the early eighteenth-century book *Gemme Antiche* by P. A. Maffei. Here the Minotaur is shown as a centaur, a form in which he was often depicted (see also 122, for example). The design of 64 is very similar. Drawings such as this were used in encyclopaedias to illustrate 'Labyrinth'. They probably all derived from the same source.

64

63

[65 *above*] The Minotaur again appears as a centaur on this sixteenth-century bronze plaquette of Italian workmanship.

[66] Badges and devices were very popular on the continent of Europe in the fourteenth century. The badge was used for publicity, but the intention of the device was to mystify, and it contained a hidden meaning. A device was composed of two parts, the picture and the motto, and the object of the two was 'that they should not be so plain as to be understood by all, nor so obscure as to require a sphinx to interpret'.[29]

Gonsalvo Perez's device, illustrated here, shows the Minotaur in the labyrinth. The motto means 'In silence and hope', and comes from 'In silentio et spe sit fortitudo nostra' – 'In quietness and in confidence shall be your strength' (Isaiah 30: 15). Perez was a Spanish ecclesiastic and he used this device when he was secretary to Emperor Charles V at Naples.

Bois-Dofin de Laval, Archbishop of Embrun, had a device with a labyrinth, and the motto 'Fata viam invenient' – 'Fate will find the way'. The same motto was used by Christina, Queen of Sweden, in her device showing a labyrinth.

## Turf Mazes

[67] Turf mazes are today associated primarily with England, just as stone mazes are thought of as Scandinavian. Both types can be found elsewhere, however, and I have details of turf mazes having existed in Germany, Italy, Sweden, and possibly in France and Iceland.

I have been able to discover only eight ancient turf mazes still surviving in England. There must have been many more in the Middle Ages, but they are easily lost, by neglect or the plough. Also, the Puritans condemned turf mazes just as they condemned maypoles and other traditional practices.

The most northerly maze to be seen today is a small one called the 'City of Troy' on the grass verge of a road near the villages of Dalby and Brandsby in the Howardian Hills of North Yorkshire.

[68] Another Yorkshire maze was that on Ripon Common, but it was, sadly, ploughed up in 1827. It was 60 feet across, and the path was 407 yards long.

[69, 70] The maze at Alkborough, North
Lincolnshire (diameter 44 feet), is set
in a depression on top of an escarpment
overlooking the plain of the River
Trent where it flows into the Humber
estuary. It is thought to have been cut
around 1200 by Benedictine monks who
lived in the village, but it may be older;
close by is a square earthwork called
the Countess Close. The design of
this maze, called 'Julian's Bower', is very
similar to that at Wing [76], and both
have a strong resemblance to the carved
maze in Lucca Cathedral [136] and
other church mazes illustrated later.

Julian's Bower was in use at least
until the beginning of the nineteenth
century, when the villagers played
May-Eve games there, 'under an indefi-
nite persuasion of something unseen
and unknown co-operating with them.'

There are three other mazes at
Alkborough, all recent and of the same
design [164–66].

[71] Lincolnshire formerly had several other turf mazes, the one on the Humber bank near Marfleet being known as the 'Walls of Troy'. Again the design is the same as that at Alkborough.

[72] Another lost maze, ploughed up in 1797 when the land was enclosed, was 'Robin Hood's Race' or 'Shepherd's Race', on a hill near St Anne's Well, Sneinton, Nottinghamshire. The design, with four corner 'bastions', is unusual, the only other similar design being the large turf maze at Saffron Walden [80]. The diameter across the circular core was 63 feet; the length of the path was 535 yards. The paths were 'circular trenches cut in the turf, scarcely a foot wide'.

One lady who remembered the maze in her childhood wrote: 'Another of my walks was to the Shepherd's Race, so-called; this was a curious labyrinth cut in the turf, supposed to have been made by the monks of St. Anne's Monastery for their amusement. We had to go through these meadows on to the Sneinton Plain. Many and many a time have I run it with great delight. It was a great shame to destroy it.'

Another Nottinghamshire maze was at Clifton, about 4 miles from Sneinton. A small plan of it can be seen beside the drawing of the former maze at Pimpern [86].

[73] The fact that some of the turf mazes were situated near churches or the houses of religious orders caused some people to think that their original purpose was purely religious, the same interpretation being placed on them as was placed on the tile mazes to be found in some continental churches. It may well be true that monks and others performed penance on the turf mazes as illustrated here, and the crosses cut out in the turf of the Sneinton maze do strengthen the religious connection in this particular case, but it is difficult to accept an ecclesiastical origin as the complete explanation, knowing that the evidence for the labyrinth goes far back into history, long before Christianity.

The maze at Sneinton was close to the chapel of St Anne, built in 1409, and one improbable explanation for this maze, offered by a Nottingham historian, Dr Deering, was: 'I should think this open maze was made by some of the priests belonging to St. Anne's chappel [sic], who being confined so far as not to venture out of sight and hearing, contrived this to give themselves a breathing for want of other exercise.'

[74] 'Caerdroia' was the name given to mazes cut out in the turf by the shepherds in the Welsh hills. There is some disagreement as to whether Caerdroia means 'City of Troy' or is the Welsh *Caer y troiau*, 'city of windings/turnings'.

In Cumberland also the herdsmen used to cut mazes in the turf, on the marshes of Burgh and Rockliffe. They called them 'Walls of Troy'.

[75] The treading of the 'Shepherd's Ring' or 'Shepherd's Race' at Boughton Green, in Northamptonshire, was a popular event in the three-day fair held every June. But this small (37 feet in diameter) maze suffered during the First World War when trenches were dug across it by soldiers in training, and it has never been restored. No trace of it now remains. Its site, half a mile from the nearest village, was close to the church of St John the Baptist, now an eery, ivy-covered ruin.

This maze design is interesting because it ends in a definite spiral. Another turf maze with a central spiral was the one on Ripon Common [68].

74

75

[76, 77] The turf maze at Wing, Rutland, is one of the few carefully preserved examples. It is small, only 40 feet in diameter, and its design is similar to other turf and church mazes. As it is fairly close to the parish church, an ecclesiastical origin has been suggested for this maze; but closer still is an ancient tumulus. The nineteenth-century plan shown here can be seen to differ slightly from the maze on the ground.

[78] There are two turf mazes still well preserved in the eastern counties, the photograph here illustrating the one at Hilton, Huntingdonshire. The message on the central obelisk states that it was laid out in 1660 by 19-year-old William Sparrow; but maybe he only recut a neglected maze.

Not far away, at Comberton, Cambridgeshire, there was until recently a turf maze called 'The Mazles' (it is described in Matthews' book *Mazes and Labyrinths*, with a photograph). Comberton is not far from Bourn, where an interesting tile maze can be seen in the church [162].

'*The lovers of antiquity, particularly of the inferior class, always speak of 'em with great pleasure and as if there was something extraordinary in the thing, tho' they cannot tell what.*' William Stukeley, speaking of turf mazes in *Itinerarium Curiosum*, 1724

[79–81] Having visited the small turf mazes at Brandsby, Alkborough, Wing and Hilton (all with diameters of around 40 feet), it is quite a surprise to come upon the maze on the common at Saffron Walden, Essex. Its diameter across the centre is approximately 90 feet – or from corner to corner, 138 feet.

It was recut several times after 1699 (when the first mention of it is made, in the Corporation account books). In the 1911 recutting, the paths were lined with bricks, which can be clearly seen in the closer photograph.

Towards the end of the eighteenth century, the maze was popular with the young men of the town, who devised a complicated system of rules and wagers. Those who walked it correctly were rewarded with beer.

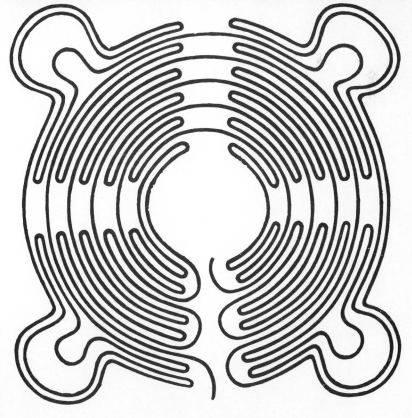

[82] The best-kept turf maze I have seen
is the 'Troy Town' at Somerton,
Oxfordshire. It measures approximately
50 feet by 60 feet, and the path is 400
yards long. This maze is in the garden
of a farmhouse also named 'Troy'.
Because it is on private property, the
owners ask that anyone wishing to
see the maze should make an appoint-
ment to do so beforehand.

[83] In the south of England, mazes are often called 'Mizmaze', and this is the name by which the maze at Breamore, Hampshire, is known. Its situation is probably the most intriguing of all the mazes, for it occupies a clearing in a small copse apparently miles from anywhere. It is approached through a wood beside the beautiful country house called Breamore House, and finding it involves a mile-long walk through remote and peaceful countryside.

This maze is quite large, its diameter being 87 feet. The central 'goal' is a raised mound 18 feet across. It takes some time to run the maze (the photograph shows the author in action), and it used to be said that a man could run from the maze to Gallows Hill (more than half a mile away) and back again while another man was running the maze.

[84] Another Mizmaze is to be seen on St Catherine's Hill, near Winchester in Hampshire. In this example, the path is along the groove rather than along the raised turf, and Matthews[30] considers that this was a misinterpretation of a plan which occurred when the maze was recut by someone who knew little about them, possibly the Warden of Winchester who is known to have recut the maze in the mid-nineteenth century. The maze, quadrangular in design, is 86 feet square.

[85] Dorset has no existing mazes, but the site of one can still be seen at Leigh. On top of a hill just outside the village is a low bank enclosing a flat area where the maze used to be. It was thirty paces in diameter, and the path was bounded by ridges about a foot wide and 6 inches high. Hutchins' *History of Dorset* (1774) comments: 'Heretofore, it was the custom for the young men of the village to scour out the trenches and pare the banks once in six or seven years, and the day appointed for the purpose was passed in rustic merriment and festivity. But of late years, either through want of encouragement . . . or from a less reverence for a curious piece of antiquity, this salutary piece of work has been neglected.' The maze was on commonland which was enclosed about 1800, and the maze was gradually obliterated until today only the surrounding bank can be seen.

Turf mazes are sometimes linked with witchcraft, and there is a local tradition that the last Dorset witch was caught performing her rites on the mizmaze at Leigh, and subsequently hanged at Maumbury Rings, Dorchester. The local Women's Institute have incorporated this story into their banner, which depicts a witch above a maze.

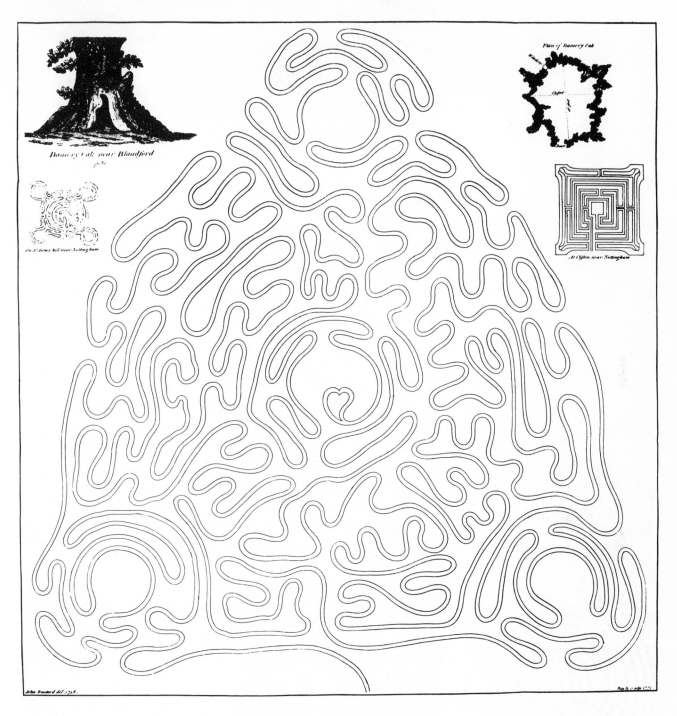

Damory Oak near Blandford

On St James bill near Nottingham

Plan of Damory Oak

At Clifton near Nottingham

John Bastard del. 1758.

[86] It is even more unfortunate that this unique turf maze at Pimpern, Dorset, has been destroyed. It covered nearly an acre of ground with foot-high ridges edging the path, and was ploughed up in 1730. The design bears no resemblance to any other turf maze, and looks almost modern. (This engraving was made from John Bastard's drawing of 1758.) John Aubrey wrote in 1686 that this maze was 'much used by the young people on Holydaies and by ye Schoolboies'.

According to Pliny the Elder,[31] turf mazes were 'made in the fields for the amusement of children' in Italy in the first century A.D. As far as I know, there are none to be seen in Italy today.

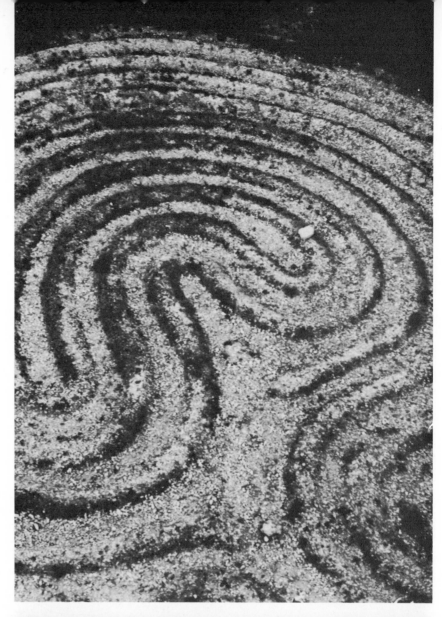

87

[87–89] Here can be seen the two best preserved turf mazes (or *Trojaburgen* – note the 'Troy' name) in Germany. Illustration 87 shows the central part of the maze at Graitschen. 88 and 89 show Steigra's maze, which stands close by a tumulus. Both mazes are in the south of East Germany.

88

89

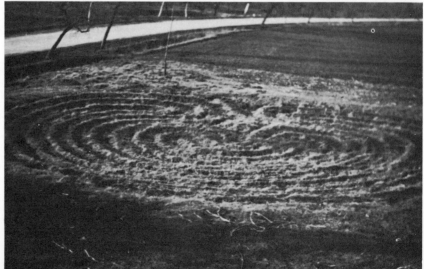

## Dances, Rituals and Games

[90] Maze dances have already been referred to in the introduction. One type of maze dance or processional parade may be illustrated on an Etruscan terracotta winejar from Tragliatella, Italy, which dates from the late seventh century B.C. A procession is depicted, led by three people who are followed by seven young men with shields on which are boars. Then come a man and woman, two horsemen with shields bearing birds, and a monkey. The whole procession emerges from, or is associated with, a maze labelled TRUIA. Behind the maze are two couples copulating.

A clue to what is happening may be found in Virgil's *Aeneid*, Book V. According to Roman tradition, Aeneas introduced the Game of Troy (*Ludus Trojae* or *Lusus Trojae*) into Italy, and his son Ascanius (Iulus) introduced it to the Romans by way of the Alban kings. Virgil's description reads, in the translation by Jackson Knight: 'The riders now moved in gay procession past the whole seated gathering in full view of their kindred ... They say that once upon a time in mountainous Crete the labyrinth contained a path twining between walls which barred the view, with a treacherous uncertainty in its thousand ways, so that its baffling plan ... would foil the trail of any guiding clues. By just such a course the sons of the Trojans knotted their paths ... Much later Ascanius inaugurated a revival of the Trojan Ride and taught the Latins to celebrate it just as he had celebrated it in his youth ... Rome in her grandeur inherited it and preserved the ancestral rite.'

This rite began as part of the funeral ceremonies performed for Anchises by the Trojans, and after its revival it continued to be performed at funerals. So again here is another association of the labyrinth with death. Jackson Knight suggests[32] that the maze movements of the Truia were intended to keep evil influences from the grave and at the same time to admit those authorized to visit it.

Robert Graves gives a different interpretation in his book *The White Goddess*.[33] He says that 'The maze pattern has been shown to represent "Spiral Castle" or "Troy Town", where the sacred sun-king goes after death and from which, if lucky, he returns' and he claims that the whole myth is presented on the winejar.

[91] In Britain there are many ancient customs and festivals still preserved, and one which might possibly have originated as a maze dance is the Abbots Bromley Horn Dance, performed every September at Abbots Bromley in Staffordshire. The dancers carry carved wooden replicas of the heads and antlers of reindeer, three sets painted white, three black, and they perform a dance in single file. Every so often the leader doubles back, after having led the others into a circle; the blacks and whites are then face to face and engage in symbolic combat, after which the procession begins again.

The meaning of this ritual dance is unknown, though it has been suggested that it may be a relic of a hunting dance. Its symbolism probably goes

far deeper, and it has also been suggested that the 'battle' signifies the struggle between life and death. The single-file twisting dance, illustrated in the photograph, has echoes of a maze dance; and the antlers and animal heads may possibly symbolize the Minotaur.

One description of the Crane Dance of Delos emphasizes its spiral nature: 'The dancers, having danced into the labyrinth from right to left, the direction of involution and death, turn round in the centre and, following their leader dance out again, now in the opposite direction, that of evolution and birth. The pattern of the spirals in the Geranos Dance signifies the continuation of life beyond death, the intimation of immortality at the very core of human experience.'[34]

Is it simply coincidence that spiral dances were once performed in Britain also? From a book of Cornish folklore[35] come descriptions of two spiral dances, one called the 'snails' creep': 'The young people being all assembled in a large meadow, the village band strikes up a simple but lively air, and marches forward, followed by the whole assemblage, leading hand-in-hand (or more closely linked in case of engaged couples), the whole keeping time to the tune with a lively step. The band or head of the serpent keeps marching in an ever-narrowing circle, whilst its train of dancing followers becomes coiled around it in circle after circle. It is now that the most interesting part of the dance commences, for the band, taking a sharp turn about, begins to retrace the circle, still followed as before, and a number of young men with long, leafy branches in their hands as standards, direct this counter-movement with almost military precision.'[36]

In the same book another Cornish spiral dance is described, called by the children who performed it 'roll-tobacco'. 'They join hands in one long line, the taller children at the head. The first child stands still, whilst the others in ever-narrowing circles dance around singing, until they are coiled into a tight mass. The outer coil then wheels sharply in a contrary direction, followed by the remainder, retracing their steps.'

J. G. Frazer associates the Cretan maze with sun-worship (mentioned earlier, see illustration 53), and of the Crane Dance says: 'May not, then, Ariadne's dance have been an imitation of the sun's course in the sky? and may not its intention have been, by means of sympathetic magic, to aid the great luminary to run his race on high? . . . If there is any truth in this conjecture, it would seem to follow that the sinuous lines of the labyrinth which the dancers followed in their evolution may have represented the ecliptic, the sun's apparent annual path in the sky.'[37]

[92] A twentieth-century revival of Morris dancing means that today groups can be seen performing in many places throughout Britain during the summer. Their rituals also are of great antiquity, probably originating as fertility dances and celebrating the death of winter and birth of spring (their first appearance is usually on May Day). There are features of their dances which may connect them with maze dances: the dancers are usually accompanied by a hobby horse, half human, half animal, and possibly a representation of the Minotaur; and the bells they wear on their legs are very similar in intention and effect to the ankle-rattles made from hollow seed pods which are worn by the *na-leng* maze dancers of Malekula when they perform maze dances at funeral rites. (For more information on Malekula, see illustrations 225–7.)

[93] Linked with the previous illustration in name if not in appearance is this carving of the 'board' for the game of nine men's morris (also known as trios, merrils, ninepenny morals, and, in the Isle of Wight, as 'siege of Troy'). This game was once very popular in Britain, the square design being cut in turf, chalked on floors, carved on tables, seats, church windowsills – anywhere in fact where people gathered together. The stone illustrated here was found at Old Sarum near Salisbury, Wiltshire. The game was not confined to Britain; the same pattern, called 'the Troy game', has also been found scratched on a window sill in the Camerlenghi Palace, Venice.

The object of this game for two was to get three of your nine counters in a row on the intersections of the lines or in the three angles of one corner.

Apart from its names 'Siege of Troy', and 'the Troy game', and the fact that the layout of the 'board' is an elementary labyrinth, nine men's morris may also be linked with labyrinths through the children's game of hopscotch, the subject of the next illustration.

[94] The name 'merrils' for nine men's morris is probably descended from the old French *jeu de merelles*, hopscotch. The layout for merrils may also be descended from hopscotch figures, of which there are a number of different designs.[38] Some versions of the game incorporate spirals or circular movements, and as hopscotch and other children's games are of great antiquity, it may be that there is here a distant echo again of maze dances. A German researcher, Frederick Hirsch, believes that children's pavement games like hopscotch are a folk-memory of pre-Christian cosmologies.[39] He says that the game symbolizes the course of the sun, and in support of this theory reports that Danish children cry 'one year old' or 'I have a year' after having completed one course of the hopscotch figure according to the children's rules.

Roger Caillois confirms the antiquity of hopscotch when he says: 'Hopscotch indeed symbolized the labyrinth through which the initiate must first wander' and 'In antiquity, hopscotch was a labyrinth in which one pushed a stone – i.e. the soul – toward the exit. With Christianity, the design became elongated and simplified, reproducing the layout of a basilica. The problem in moving the stone became to help the soul attain heaven, paradise, halo, or glory, coinciding with the high altar of the church, and schematically represented on the ground by a series of rectangles.'[40]

In Cornwall the spiral form of hopscotch was called 'snail-creep', reminding one of the spiral dance 'snails'-creep' described earlier [91].

[95] Mazes called 'Walls of Troy' were drawn on the sand of Scottish beaches (and probably in other places too) as late as the 1920s, as a game for children, the game being, of course, running in procession to the centre and out again.

The sand maze shown here was drawn on the beach in the Isle of Wight by John Barnatt and Ken Beagley [267].

[96] A maze game in modern dress is 'aMaze', a puzzle made of moulded polystyrene by Design Objectives Ltd. It has a transparent cover, and inside is a small ball. The object is to guide the ball to the centre of the maze by tipping the board from side to side. Games of this kind were also popular in Victorian times [245].

[97] Another modern puzzle based on the maze is this transparent plastic cube. It is divided into sixty-four smaller cubes by transparent partitions, some of which are missing, and the object is to navigate a marble dropped into the hole on top, through the maze and out of the hole at the bottom.

[98] Over the years several books of maze puzzles have been published, and these retain their popularity. This puzzle comes from a recent book (*Greg Bright's Maze Book*) in which the puzzles progress from the straightforward to the extremely difficult, and the point in this example is to get from the gap at the bottom to the tiny diamond directly above it.

## Mazes of Stones

[99] Just as turf mazes seem to be peculiar to England, so mazes of stones are found largely in Scandinavia. There are many, many examples, made of stones and boulders of varying sizes, and the majority seem to be in Sweden. Though other Scandinavian countries less well explored may also possess excellent examples known only to the local people.

Perhaps Sweden's best-known stone maze is one on the island of Gotland, which is in the Baltic Sea off the east coast of the mainland. This maze, known as Trojeborg (Troy Castle), is on flat ground below Gallow's Hill near Visby. One explanation for its presence there is that it was built by a girl in the Middle Ages, in order to obtain a pardon for her rich pirate father. She promised the Council of Visby that she would promote the area's tourist industry (to use modern terminology) by building a marvellous construction that people would come from far and wide to see.

[100, 101] Also on Gotland, there is a maze in the grass by Fröjel church. This was excavated and restored in May 1974 by Stig Englund, and the photographs show the maze before and after restoration.

[102] This aerial view shows a clearly
defined maze at Lindbacke, St Nikolai
parish, Södermanland province, in south-
east Sweden.

[103] South-west Sweden is the location
of this maze which looks as though
its stones are beginning to disperse. It is
one of four on the island of Ramnö
in Onsala parish, province of Halland.

[104] Again in Halland, this time at Yttre Lön in Olmevalla parish. Most stone mazes are by the sea. W. F. Jackson Knight suggested that they may have been located there because sailors performed maze rituals before going to sea. The dead 'had once started across the sea on their journey', and the sailors, going from the realm of life into the realm of death, were guarding against possible dangers in this unknown realm 'by entering it ceremoniously through the doors of the "house of death", the labyrinth'.[41]

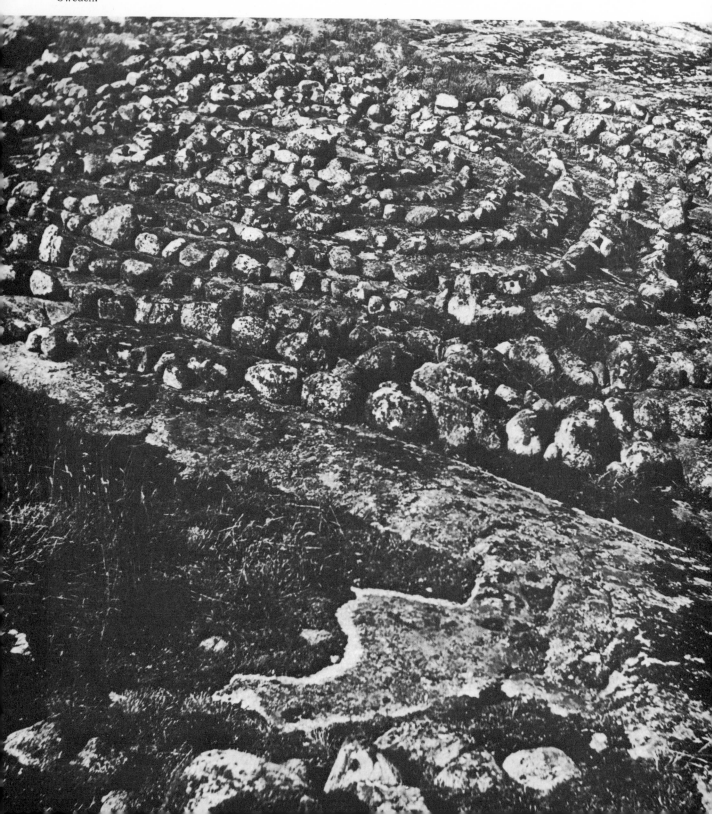

[105] The boulders are weathered and
lichen-covered, blended into the landscape, in this photograph of the maze at
Koholmen near Vinga, in Styrsö
parish, Bohuslän province, in south-west
Sweden.

[106] This interesting aerial view shows the maze at Tibble in Badelunda parish, Västmanland province, in south-east Sweden.

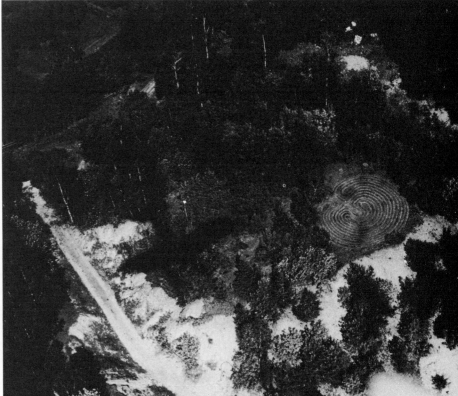

[107] Sweden is not the only country, however, where stone labyrinths are to be found. According to Matthews' *Mazes and Labyrinths*, they can (or could) also be found in Lappland, Finland and Norway. There were also mazes in Iceland, sometimes of stone, sometimes of earth, and these were called *Völundarhús*, or Wayland's House. Most of them were in the north-west of the country, and at one time were used as a fishermen's pastime, but sadly almost all have now disappeared.

The illustration shows the maze on Wier Island in the Gulf of Finland, as discovered by Dr E. von Baer in 1838.

Away from Scandinavia, a spiral boulder labyrinth constructed of small stones was found a century ago in India. A more precise location, for

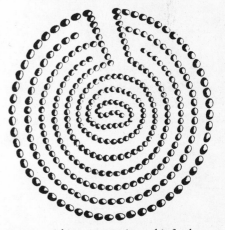

anyone wishing to investigate this further, is: near the site of the ruined city of Kundani, in Hosur Taluq, Salem District, Madras Presidency, near the Baire Gauni tank, on the hill south of Devar-Kundani.[42]

[108, 109] A stone maze can still be seen on one of the smaller Scilly Isles off Cornwall, St Agnes. It was said locally that it was constructed in 1726 by a lighthouse keeper from London, but he was probably only renewing an earlier structure.

The photographs show the 'Troy Town' in 1885, with the wreck of the *Earl of Lonsdale* in the background; and the site on the occasion of a royal visit in May 1921.

[110] This 'tourist's maze' is on St Martin's, again in the Scilly Isles.

## Roman Mosaics

[111] The Romans are famed for their
mosaic pavements, and they often
incorporated many intricate designs. The
labyrinth is sometimes seen, and the
selection of pictures which follows contains examples from all over Europe.

The elaborate mosaic illustrated here
was found in a Roman villa near
Salzburg, Austria. It is 18 feet long by
15 feet wide, and at the centre Theseus
can be seen dealing the death blow to the
Minotaur.

[112] This pavement was discovered at Cormerod in the Canton of Friburg, Switzerland, in 1830.

[113] Discovered at Saint-Côme-et-Maruéjols (Gard) in southern France, this mosaic measures 3 feet 6 inches wide by 5 feet 3 inches deep.

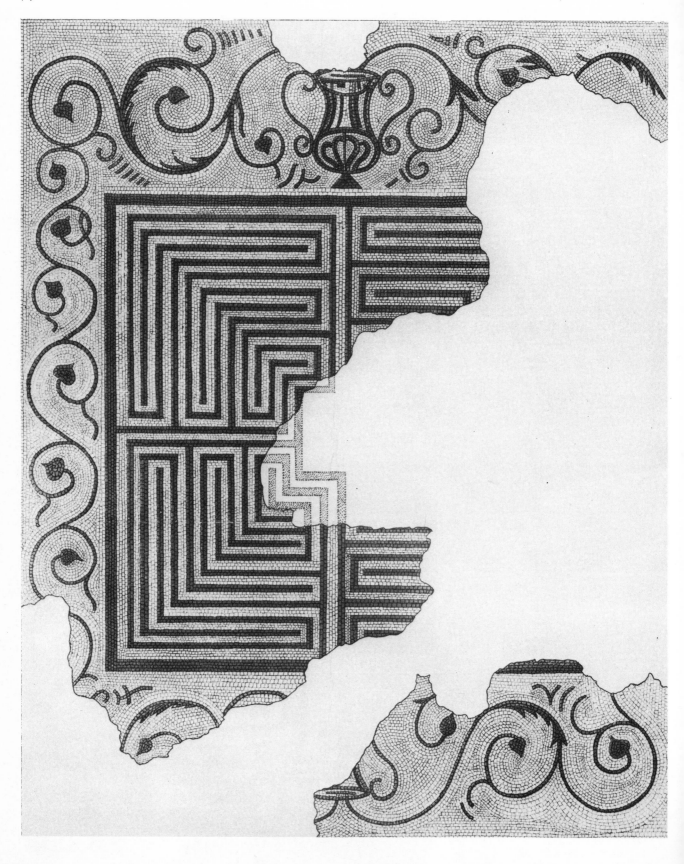

[114 *left*] A damaged mosaic pavement with a labyrinth design was discovered in the churchyard at Caerleon, South Wales, in 1866.

[115] In 1904 a large pavement, measuring approximately 16 feet 6 inches by 17 feet 6 inches, was discovered during the excavation of a Roman villa at Harpham in the East Riding of Yorkshire. The pavement, now restored, is on display on a wall by the staircase in the City Hall, Kingston upon Hull.

Anyone following this maze will be disappointed to discover that it does not work. Something has gone wrong, possibly during restoration, in the bottom righthand sector. The corner nearest the centre is different from the others, and there should not be a gap through into the horizontal passage which leads to the centre.

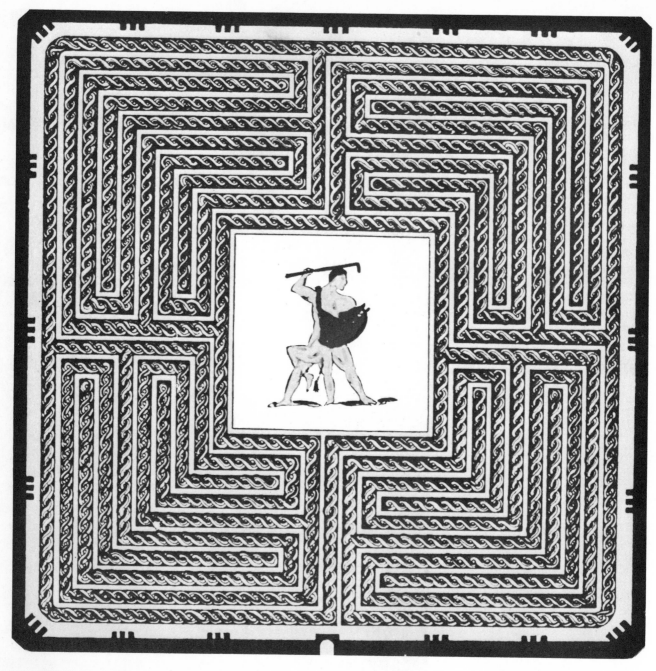

[116] This labyrinth is in a Roman villa
at Italica, just over 6 miles from
Seville, Spain.

[117] Theseus is seen sailing away, leaving the Minotaur dead, at the centre of this mosaic labyrinth which was discovered in the late nineteenth century on a tomb at Susa in Tunis. It was destroyed by looters, but not before this careful drawing had·been made. The mosaic measured about 17 feet by 10 feet.

[118] This recently discovered (1959) mosaic is in Italy. It was found at Calvatone, which is near Piadena, near Cremona.

[119] Pompeii, the Italian town buried in
lava during the eruption of Vesuvius
in A.D. 79, has a House of the Labyrinth,
named because of its pictorial references to the Cretan labyrinth. The labyrinth pavement illustrated was found
in the Villa of Diomede.

[120] Another Italian mosaic labyrinth, this time discovered in 1957 in the Via Cadolini, Cremona. The centre depicts Theseus killing the Minotaur.

## Manuscripts, Books and Maps – 11th to 18th centuries

[121 *right*] The manuscript from which this drawing comes is of eleventh-century Visigothic origin (the Visigoths were the western Goths with settlements in the south of France and Spain); the manuscript contains the *Etymologies* of Isidore of Seville. The labyrinth is in the middle of a section on Easter, and opposite is a short passage in Spanish on the Epistles of St Paul.

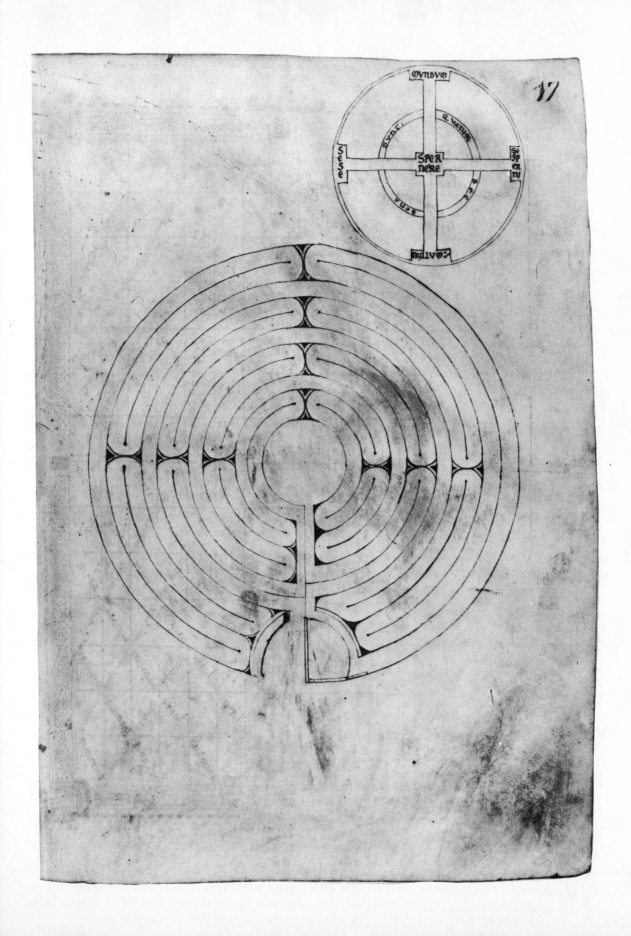

DOMDOE INA MEAVRBSIW

MYNOS REX.

DEDALVS
Artifex

YCARVS
filiuf ei;

Pasiphe
regina

minotaur
inlaberincho

Asiphe regina creientium concubuit cu tauro induta uacca lignea qua dedalus imperia sua
composuerat concepit ex eo peperitq; minotauru semi uiru & semiboue; Quo uiro dedalus ex praecepto
minois regis sua fouea scilicet laberinthu denique desuper posita; est ut minotauru; Deuicere sub
mensib; a minos rex creienti statuerat illi sibi dari hoc tributu ut semp post tres annos bis septe corpora
iuuenu errore in uitta; Minos rex maior aduersus dedalu; tu agere impune facto

[122 *left*] The Minotaur inside the labyrinth is the subject of this illustration
from the *Liber Floridus* of Lambert of
Saint-Omer (*c.* 1120).

[123, 124] A worried-looking Theseus
faces a savage snarling Minotaur
inside a labyrinth from the thirteenth-
century *De VII Miraculis Mundi*
(Regensburg, Germany, 1175–1200).

From the same manuscript comes
a labyrinth (*above*) which its designer has
captioned: 'The city of Jericho was a
similar shape to the moon.' Jill Purce
comments: 'To the ancients, the labyrinth was a part of founding a town:
cutting off a portion of space and
transforming it from chaos into cosmos.
The windings which laid the foundation also protected it from entry of all
but those with knowledge, the
knowledge of the way.'[43]

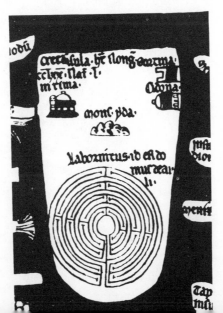

[125 *left*] The 'Mappa Mundi' is one of
the earliest English maps and dates from
the thirteenth century. It was made by
Richard Hallingdon of Battle, Sussex,
who was a prebendary of Hereford, and
the map can be seen today in Hereford
Cathedral. It is full of wonders and
fabulous creatures, but the interesting feature for us is the labyrinth which
half-fills the island of Crete. It is
inscribed 'Labarintus id est domus
Dealli'.

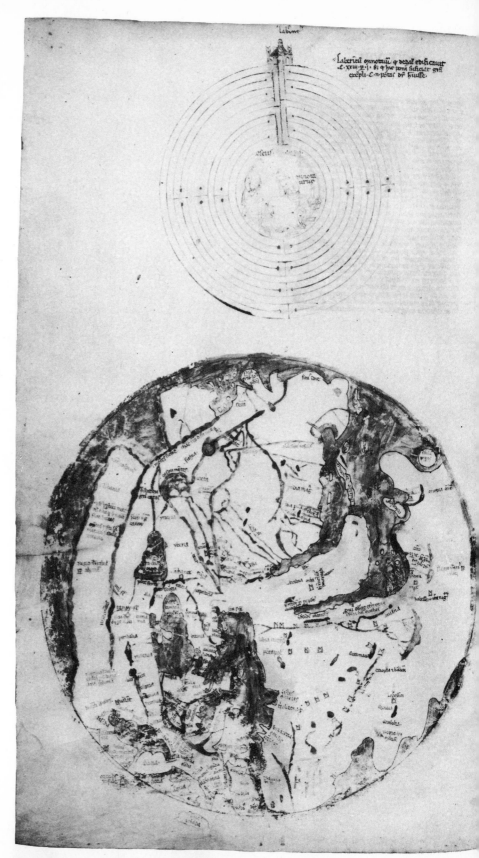

[126] A fourteenth-century manuscript
in the Vatican Library contains a
labyrinth with, at the centre, Theseus
apparently clubbing the Minotaur
(who is depicted as a centaur, and holds
his head in apparent bewilderment).

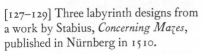

[127–129] Three labyrinth designs from
a work by Stabius, *Concerning Mazes*,
published in Nürnberg in 1510.

[130] This knot design is labyrinthine in effect, if the pattern is followed round. The design comes from *Sechs Knoten* by Albrecht Dürer (1471–1528). Leonardo da Vinci (1462–1519) also produced knot labyrinths (concatenations). In an article on

Dürer's 'knots' and Leonardo's 'concatenations', Ananda K. Coomaraswamy concluded that the labyrinth and the knots are identical: 'That the lines of the knots are superposed and intersect involves no difference in principle, but represents a translation of the idea of the maze into three-dimensional terms.'[44]

[131] An island labyrinth, approached only over a ramshackle bridge, is the subject of this sixteenth-century engraving by Hieronymus Cook. This labyrinth resembles very closely the illustration from Ovid's *Metamorphoses* [58].

[132] Seventeenth-century Poland is the source of this cabbalistic labyrinth used by Polish magician Isak Lurje.

[133] This alchemical drawing shows the Lapis Sanctuary, within a labyrinth and surrounded by the planetary orbits. (*Lapis philosophicus* is the philosopher's stone.) The drawing comes from *De Groene Leeuw* by Goosen van Vreeswyk (Amsterdam, 1672).

## Churches and Cathedrals in Algeria, Italy, France and Scandinavia

[134] Possibly the oldest church maze is in the Church of Reparatus, Orléans-ville, in Algeria. The church itself dates from the fourth century A.D., and the maze, 8 feet in diameter, is in the pavement near the north-west entrance. The centre contains the words SANCTA ECLESIA, which can be read in any direction starting from the centre (but not diagonally).

[136 *right*] One of the smallest Italian church mazes is that carved on the wall of Lucca Cathedral. Its diameter is only 1 foot 7½ inches. Theseus and the Minotaur could at one time be seen in the centre, but the fingers of centuries have rubbed them away. The Latin inscription on the right reads when translated: 'This is the labyrinth which the Cretan Daedalus built, out of which nobody could get who was inside, except Theseus; nor could he have done it, unless he had been helped with a thread by Adriane, all for love.'

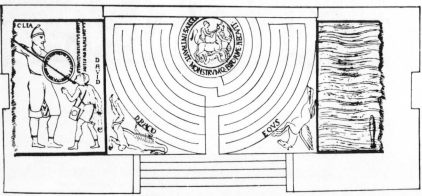

[135] Several Italian churches and cathedrals possess mazes, and there is a small one on the wall inside the church of San Michele Maggiore, Pavia, Italy. It may have been made during the tenth century A.D.

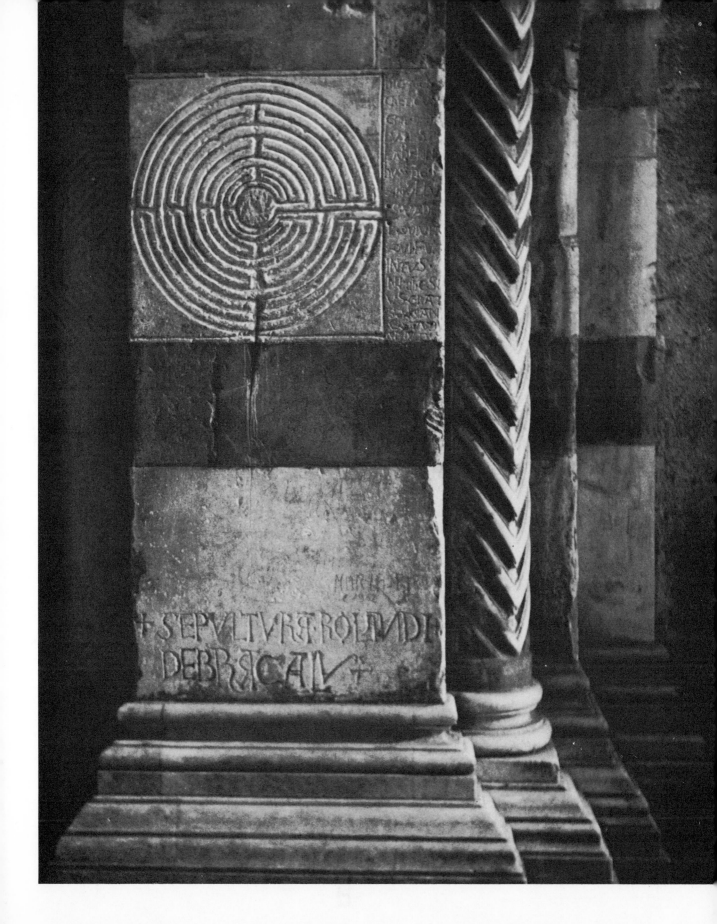

[137] The church of Sta Maria-in-Aquiro, Rome, has a maze 5 feet in diameter. A central plate of porphyry is surrounded by bands of porphyry and yellow and green marble.

[138] Also in Rome, there is a maze of coloured marble in the church of Sta Maria-di-Trastavera. It is 11 feet in diameter and may at some time have been incorrectly repaired because it is not possible to follow the path to the centre. This maze has been dated to the end of the twelfth century A.D.

[139] The maze in the sixth-century church of San Vitale, Ravenna, Italy, is almost 11½ feet in diameter, and is composed of coloured marble.

[140, 141] The church-builders of medie-val France incorporated mazes into a number of churches and cathedrals, but only a few have been preserved. The largest and best-known is in Chartres Cathedral. Originally called 'La Lieue' (which usually meant 'the league', its significance in this case being unknown), it is about 40 feet in diameter and constructed of blue and white· stones. The verses of the psalm 'Miserere' were engraved on the white stone of the path to be followed.

A plan of the maze is preserved in the sketchbook of Villard de Honne-court, who was an architect in thirteenth-century France. He was active around 1235, during the period when

Chartres Cathedral was completed. His sketchbook is described by Robert Branner in *Gothic Architecture*:[45] 'Villard seems to have begun the manuscript as a sketchbook and then to have turned it into a manual for the guidance of apprentices, adding explanatory phrases and directions to the drawings. Along with ground plans, elevations, and views of monuments, he sketched church furnishings, such as choir stalls, a lectern, and a great clock case. He also copied sculpture and perhaps even some images from stained glass, and he was fascinated by nature, drawing pictures of insects and animals.'

At the beginning of his sketchbook the architect wrote: 'Villard de Honnecourt greets you and begs all those who may use in their work the devices which they find in this book to pray for his soul and remember him. For in this book good advice can be found on the noble art of the mason, on the craft of carpentry, and . . . on the uses of drawing which the study of geometry demands and teaches.'

A recent paper[46] presents evidence suggesting that Chartres maze can be interpreted as an image of the cosmos; it also illustrates the importance of the positioning of the maze within the cathedral. The following is a short extract from the paper: 'So what we have implied is the body of the cathedral reflecting a reconciliation between Lunar and Solar cycles and the psychological forces of which they are the physical embodiments. This act of hingeing the elevation down on to the ground plan points to the significance of the positioning of the maze. The great twelve-fold west rose window not only conforms basically in size to the maze, but when hinged down on to the floor of the nave covers it almost exactly.' The same paper also explains the symbolism in following the maze: 'The individual . . . was in fact re-enacting the "descent of the soul" into manifestation in earth (the centre). One of the psychological functions of traversing the maze, apparently being to re-enact the contributing factors to the structure of one's personality.' (This idea is then expanded.)

[142] One of France's lost mazes was in Arras Cathedral. It was a pavement maze about $34\frac{1}{2}$ feet in diameter, of blue and yellow squares, and was destroyed during the French Revolution.

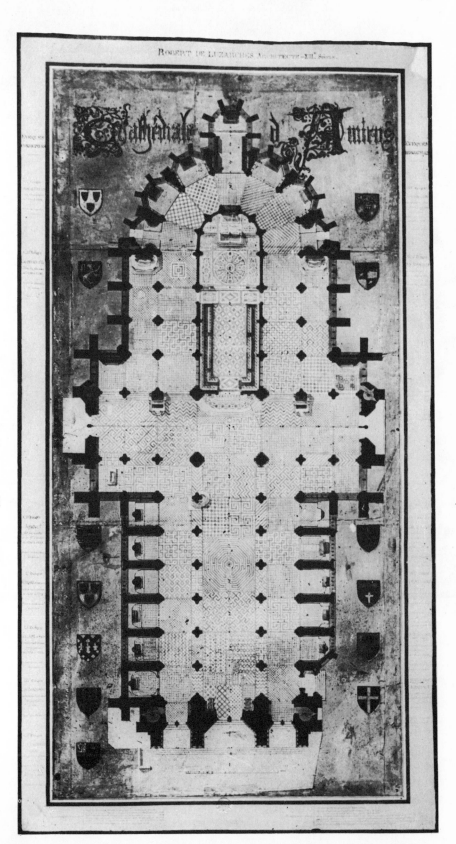

[143] The maze in Amiens Cathedral, 42 feet in diameter and dating from the late thirteenth century, was destroyed in 1825 and a copy laid in its place. The central plate contained a bronze cross and the figures of the bishop (Bishop Evrard de Fouilloy) who laid the foundation stone in 1220, and the three master-masons concerned in building the cathedral.

[144] The maze in the entrance to the
parish church of St Quentin, France, is
still in existence, and in good condition,
as is shown by the photograph. It is
34½ feet in diameter.

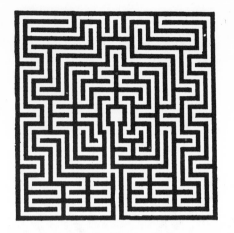

[145] The Abbey of St Bertin, in St Omer, France, is now ruined, but it once contained a pavement maze which was destroyed in the eighteenth century.

[146] An unusual maze was once to be seen in Poitiers Cathedral, France. The design is unusual in that the path does not lead to a centre or goal, but only returns to the outside.

[147] The maze in Rheims Cathedral, France, had the names and professional symbols of the thirteenth-century 'masters of the works' recorded in the corner panels. In the centre Archbishop de Humbert, who laid the foundation stone in 1211, was probably recorded.

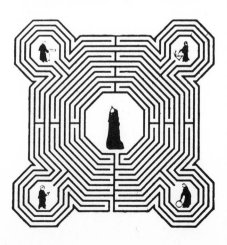

It is not known for certain as the panel was illegible by the seventeenth century. The 500-year-old maze, 35 feet in diameter, was wantonly destroyed in 1779 because one Canon Jacquemart did not like the noise made by the children and others who followed its course during services.

That the church mazes originally did have a role to play in church procedure, rather than just being a potential nuisance, is shown by the fact that the pelota ball-game or dance was performed annually on Easter Day on the maze in Auxerre Cathedral, France (destroyed at the end of the seventeenth century). The dean and canons danced in a long chain around the maze, the ball or *pilota* being handed along the line of dancers. The *pilota* was circulated round the dancers and back to the dean, and it has been suggested that 'The probable symbolism of the Pelota dance is the representation of the apparent path or dance of the sun throughout the year, its "Passion", and the corresponding Passion of creation, analogous to the path of the incarnate Christ, his death, burial and resurrection as the Christ-Sun at Easter.'[47]

[148] The chapter house of Bayeux Cathedral, France, has a maze of ornamented tiles which is 12 feet in diameter. The tiles are red, black and encaustic, with a pattern of brown and yellow, and the designs are shields, griffins and fleurs-de-lis.

[149] The maze in Sens Cathedral, France, was destroyed in 1769. It was 30 feet in diameter, and the pattern was of incised lines filled with lead.

[150] Toussaints Abbey, Châlons-sur-Marne, France, had a series of tiles decorated with mazes. The abbey was destroyed in 1544.

[151] Not until 1954 did the maze of Genainville church, Val-d'Oise, France, come to light. It is carved on a piece of stone and measures 2 feet 3 inches by 2 feet 6 inches.

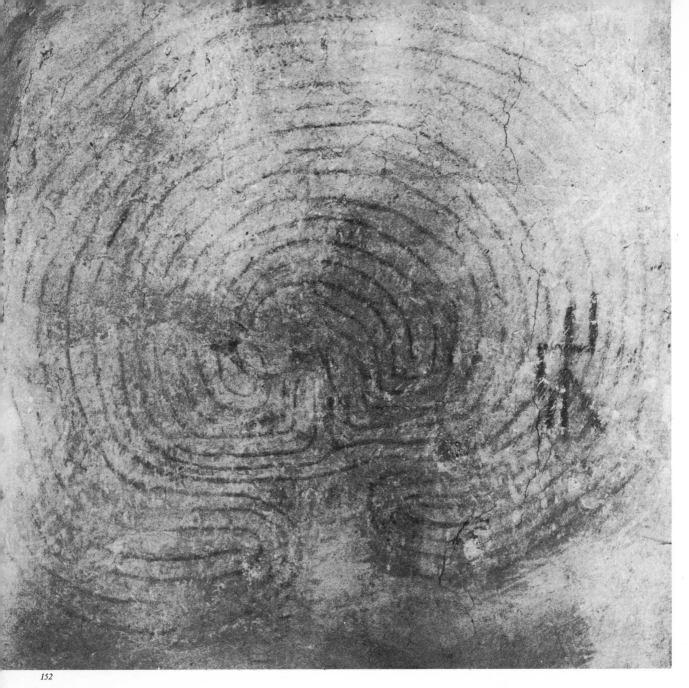

*152*

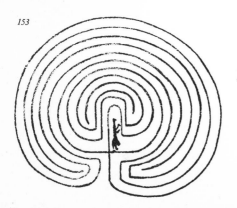

*153*

[152–156]
This barely discernible maze design [152]
was found on a wall of the tower in
Hablingbo church, on the island of
Gotland, Sweden. Similar designs
are found throughout Scandinavia: for
example, 153 is on the church wall in
Sibbo, Finland; 154 is painted on the
wall of a church in Telemark, Norway;
155 is in Gerninge church, Zealand,
Denmark (where two labyrinths are
painted on the choir-wall over the vaults);
and 156 is in Skive Old church,
Jutland, Denmark.

154

155 156

## Churches and Cathedrals in Britain

[157–159] There are very few mazes in
the churches of Britain. I came across
this one by accident, when exploring
the church of St Martin in the village of
Lewannick, which is close to the eastern
edge of Bodmin Moor, Cornwall.
Each face of an octagonal font carries a
geometric design, all of them attrac-
tive and interesting, but the two which
leapt out at me were a tightly coiled
spiral and a simple maze with a cross at
its centre. The font is old, dating back
to Norman times, and is made of local
Hicks Mills grey stone.

[160] St Mary Redcliffe church in Bristol
has a very small maze which is easily
missed if you do not know where to look
for it. Only 4 inches across, it is
carved on one of the roof bosses in the
north aisle, near the north transept.
It dates from the fifteenth century.

[161] The exact date of this simple spiral
maze, in Thornton church, Leicester-
shire, is unknown, but it is thought to be
pre-Reformation. Large stones form
a squared-off spiral leading to a centre
now containing several bricks. These,
like the brick floor of the church, were
later additions; renovation work at
the time of writing may reveal clues to
the maze's early history.

[162] As far as I can discover, there are only two pavement mazes in British churches (in contrast with the many that did or still do exist in the churches and cathedrals of France and Italy). One of them is to be found in the church of St Helena and St Mary in the quiet rural village of Bourn, Cambridgeshire. Formed of red and black tiles, it occupies the area below the tower.

and his comments on the psychological effect of this and on mazes in general are worth quoting here.

'The experience of the labyrinth, whether as a pictorial design, a dance, a garden path or a system of corridors in a temple, always has the same psychological effect. It temporarily disturbs rational conscious orientation to the point that . . . the initiate is "confused" and symbolically "loses his way". Yet in this descent to chaos the inner mind is opened to the awareness of a new cosmic dimension of a transcendent nature.

'Just inside the west portal entering the nave of Ely Cathedral in England there is, set in the stone, a large mosaic designed as a maze. I myself once followed this maze, slowly walking through it in and out or following it with my eyes from beginning to end with the striking discovery that my mental threshold was lowered, not just through dizziness, but in such a way that when I emerged from out the maze I could respond more naturally, more genuinely to the beauty of the great church beyond. While this is but a reminiscence of the ancient patterns of death and rebirth enacted in the ritual dances of antiquity or in contemporary tribal societies, its message is still authentic when it comes with a sense of renewal from within.'[48]

[163 below] The other pavement maze in Britain can be found beneath the west tower of Ely Cathedral, again in East Anglia. The distance from the entrance of the maze to the centre is the same as the height of the west tower, 215 feet. This maze is of recent origin, forming part of Sir Gilbert Scott's restoration work on the cathedral in 1870.

Jungian analyst Dr Joseph L. Henderson experienced temporary confusion and loss of orientation when he walked through the maze at Ely,

[164–166] The village of Alkborough in Lincolnshire, home of a surviving turf maze [69], also possesses three others. They are all of the same design, but none the less interesting for that. One is cut into the stone of the church porch [164]; another very small replica in blue is in the Victorian stained-glass window behind the church altar [165]; and the third is in the village cemetery, set into the tombstone of Mr J. Goulton-Constable [166], squire of the village until his death in 1922. He was interested in local history and made sure that the turf maze was kept in good order.

## Mazes and Labyrinths
## in Paint and Script

[167, 168] Occasionally (but surprisingly
rarely, considering the widespread
appearances of mazes and labyrinths in
other forms) mazes and labyrinths
are illustrated in paintings. Pre-1900
examples are shown here; for modern
paintings see illustrations 247–250.

A mural in the Sala dei Cavalli,
Palazzo Ducale, Mantua, Italy, depicts
'Olympus in the Midst of a Labyrinth'. This painting has been attributed
to the School of Lorenzo Leonbruno,
and dated to the early sixteenth century.
The labyrinth and Olympus were
both emblems of the Gonzaga family,
who were insatiable collectors and
builders and possessed many luxurious
dwellings in Italy.

Illustration 168 shows another design
from a palace belonging to the Gonzaga family. This repeated labyrinth
design decorates the floor of the Sala
di Psiche in the Palazzo de Te, Mantua.

[169] This scene from the story of David
and Bathsheba, entitled 'A King
Receiving a Deputation in the Gardens
of a Palace', is by Jan van Amstel. A
gloomy and uninviting maze can be seen
in the centre, middle distance.

[170] Hampton Court Palace near London, in whose gardens is Britain's best-known hedge maze [207], also has a painting of a maze on display. Allegedly by Tintoretto, it shows a verdant sixteenth-century landscape dominated by a hedge maze whose facilities are being enjoyed by a number of people.

[171 *left*] Labyrinth symbols were sometimes displayed on the robes of Roman emperors. This painting shows, not an emperor, but a sixteenth-century gentleman who wears a labyrinth prominently displayed on his chest. It may signify secrecy. His garments are decorated with 'Solomon's Knots', a design which combines labyrinth, cross and swastika and is known as the 'emblem of divine inscrutability'. These knots here emphasize the secrecy suggested by the central labyrinth. The painting is by Bartolommeo Veneto (*fl.* 1502–30) and has been dated to around 1510. Charles R. Beard has attempted to identify the gentleman, and he suggests that he was a Seigneur de Boisdauphin, possibly François de Laval.[49]

[172] This 'Portrait of a Gentleman' is believed to be by Dosso Dossi, and the style of the portrait indicates a date of around 1520. The man portrayed may be Angelo Perondoli, according to Felton Gibbons, because a pear was his family emblem, and there is a small pear near the figure's hand. Other significant features of this picture are the labyrinth, the ass with dead game birds slung across its back, and the stormy weather. Part of Mr Gibbons' interpretation of the painting is as follows:

'It is, I feel, in a rather conservative and still quite Christian sense that Dosso uses the labyrinth as the chief concern of his moody sitter. Here was a man, be he Angelo Perondoli or another, beset with troubles, fallen into a brown study of the web of his affairs and the storm over the landscape of his life. Even the near-monochromatic colours of the painting, unusually dun for the glistening palette of Dosso, reflect this sombre mood. If the portrayed's pointed indication of the labyrinth suggests that his life was confused by the presence of many fruitless ways, the ass may specify one of the sins that beset him, namely avarice ... Dosso in his richly impressionistic landscape subtly suggests that human endeavour and the tortured Christian way can overcome the tempests of life, for even as rain still falls and reddish lightning streaks the sky on the right, a late sun seems about to burst through the clouds on the left where the sitter himself is.'[50]

[173] Johann Caspar Hiltensperger
(*d.* 1754) produced this elaborate 'word
labyrinth', with its text from the first
chapter of the book of Jesus Sirach,
beginning: 'Alle Weissheit ist bey Gott
dem Herrn unnd ist bey Ihm ewigk-
lich . . .'

[174] This bilingual 'spiritual labyrinth' with four 'goals' containing Biblical references is in French and German, and is dated 1758.

Of the firſte Maze. Cap.v.

Here by the way (gentle Reader) I do place two proper Mazes, the one before this chapter, and the other after, as proper adornments vpon pleaſure to a Garden, that who ſo liſteth, hauing ſuche roomth in their Garden, may place the one of thē, which liketh them beſt, in that voide place of the Garden that maye beſte be ſpared, for the onelye purpoſe, to ſporte them in at times, which Mazes being workmanly handled by the Gardner, ſhal muche beautifie them, in deuiſing four ſundry fruits to be placed in each of the corners of the Maze, and in the middle of it, a proper Herber decked with Roſes, or elſe ſome faire trée of Roſemary, or other fruite, at the diſcretion of the Gardener.

¶ Of the dung and dunging of Gardens, with the digging, dreſſing, leuelling & diſpoſing of the quarters and beds. Cap.vj.

For ſo muche as in the Harueſt and Spring time, be many thinges ſowne in the Garden, therefore it behoueth to dig vp, dung, and labor that part of the ground in the Spring time, which you intend to ſowe in the Harueſt, that the ſame may ſo
ſerue

**Hedge and Garden Mazes –
Plans and Engravings**

[175, 176] By the sixteenth century, it had become very fashionable to plant herbs, flower beds or dwarf shrubs in elaborate designs, and often mazes were constructed. Later, mazes of hedges became more popular than what I call for simplicity's sake 'garden mazes'. Some of the plans which follow date from a time when both hedge and garden mazes were in vogue, and it is not always clear which kind the designs represent.

Two early plans for garden mazes can be found in *The Profitable Art of Gardening* by Thomas Hyll. This edition was published in 1579; an earlier edition published in 1563 was called *A Moste Briefe and Pleasaunt Treatyse Teachynge How to Dress, Sowe and Set a Garden*. Thomas Hyll (also Hill) was the same person as Didymus (=Thomas) Mountaine (=Hill), and under this authorship the same book appeared yet again as *The Gardener's Labyrinth*.

## Of the second Maze.  Cap.vij.

And here I also place the other Maze, which may be lyke
ordered and vsed, as I spake before, and it may eyther be
set with Isope and Time, or with winter Sauery and Tyme:
For these do wel endure, al ý winter through gréene. And there
be some which set their Mazes with Lauender Cotten, Spike,
Mairome, and such like. But let them be ordered in this point,
as liketh best the Gardener, and so an end. For I doe not here
set forth this, or the other Maze afore expressed, for any necessarie
commoditie in a Garden, but rather appoint eyther of
these (which liketh you best) as a beautifying vnto your Garden:
For that Mazes and knots aptly made, do much set forth a
Garden, which neuerthelesse I referre to your discretion for
that not all persons be of like abilitie.

¶ Certaine precepts, and rules of auntient men, both in the
choyse and proper sowing of seedes.  Cap.viij.

The Garden, as Palladius writeth, whiche lyeth vnder a
gentle and holesome ayre, and hath a fountaine, Spring,

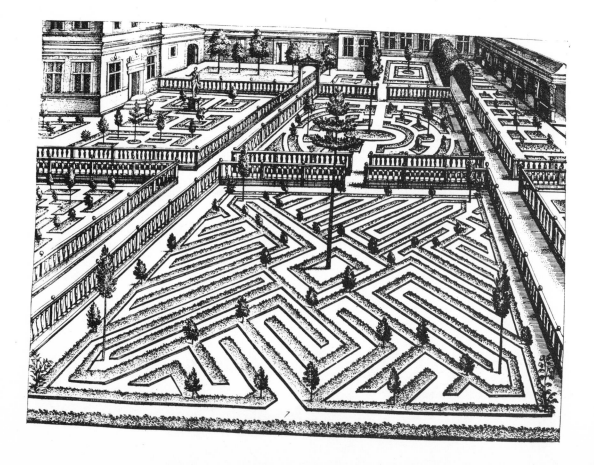

[177] The garden at the Villa d'Este, Tivoli, was said to be the finest Renaissance garden in Europe. It was begun in 1549 by Pirro Ligorio for Cardinal Ippolito the Younger, and this illustration, showing four mazes, dates from 1573.

[178–180 *below & opposite*] These three designs for garden mazes are by Jan Vredeman de Vries, and they come from his book *Hortorum Viridariorumque Formae*, published in Antwerp in 1583.

[181] This sixteenth-century engraving shows the uses a hedge maze could be put to – duelling, making music, courting, talking, strolling . . .

*Secundi generis* Fig. I.

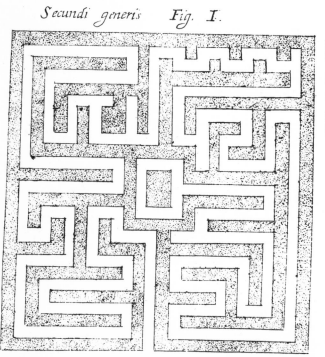

SECVNDI GENERIS FIG. II.

*Secundi generis Fig. III.*

*II. Generis Fig: IV.*

TERTII GENERIS FIG. I.
LABYRINTHVS

III. GENER. FIG. IV.
LABYRINTHVS.

[182–187] Petri Laurembergii's book
*Horticultura*, published in Frankfurt
in 1632, contains a number of designs
for mazes, of which these are a selection.

[188] Romain de Hooge's engraving of
1685 shows the maze and fountains
designed for the Parc d'Enghien,
Belgium.

[189] The maze at Versailles was constructed near the end of the seventeenth century for Louis XIV. It contained thirty-nine groups of statues which were also fountains, and these depicted the characters of Aesop's fables. The plan shows where the statues were positioned. Unfortunately this maze was destroyed in 1775. In England the Dial Garden at Friar Park, Henley-on-Thames, was laid out on the same plan with sundials in place of statues, but this too no longer exists.

[190, 191] Typical of the elaborate
designs which were being produced
in France in the seventeenth century are
these two. One shows the maze
constructed at Choisy-le-Roi, the other
shows an unidentified maze with
secluded corners and fountains. Designs
of this type are far removed from the
traditional Cretan labyrinth!

[192–195] Slightly more 'traditional' are these designs, also from France.

The designs illustrated on these pages are only a small selection of the mazes both planned on paper and actually constructed during this period of approximately 200 years. More are illustrated and/or described in W. H. Matthews' *Mazes and Labyrinths*.

[196 *below*] Hedge mazes were most prolific in Europe, but they did some-times stray to other continents, such as this example which was laid out in the early eighteenth century at the Emperor's Summer Palace, Yüan Ming

Yüan, China. Father Benoit of the Jesuit Mission was responsible for this translation of a typically European architectural feature to an alien land-scape, but this maze was completely neglected after the Emperor's death.

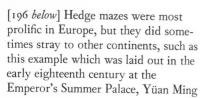

[197 *right*] As the eighteenth century dawned there seems to have been no lessening in the interest in mazes as gar-den features. This plate from Batty Langley's *New Principles of Gardening* (1728) shows an extremely elaborate garden. There is one maze proper, and the three other quarters of the plan contain designs which have obviously developed from the maze idea.

[198] Hieronymus Sperling's (1695–1777)
illustration for 'Tenet error amantem'
from Ovid's *Metamorphoses*.

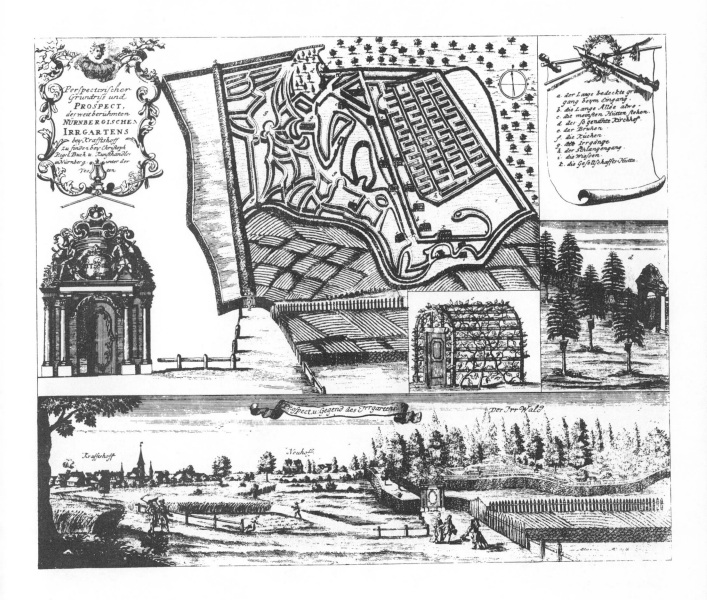

[199] Plans and designs for mazes also
originated in Germany, like this one
engraved by Johann Oswald Berndt
(1736–87). The illustration shows the
*Irrgarten* (literally 'err-garden') at
Kraftshof near Nürnberg. The tree
maze was laid out in 1676 by the Kraftshof priest, Martin Limburger.

A. Berceau med 6 Døre.
B. Salon med 8 Døre.
C. Boudoir.
D. Culs de sac.
E. Indgangen.

[200] The Tivoli Gardens in Vienna,
Austria.

[201, 202] There is a hedge maze at Stra, in Italy, 18 miles south of Venice. It is in the garden of the Villa Pisani and was constructed in the mid-eighteenth century. This maze with its imposing central observation tower topped by a statue of Minerva has 4 miles of paths, and used to be visited by around 200,000 tourists every year. Unfortunately the hedges are now overgrown, and the maze is closed to the public.

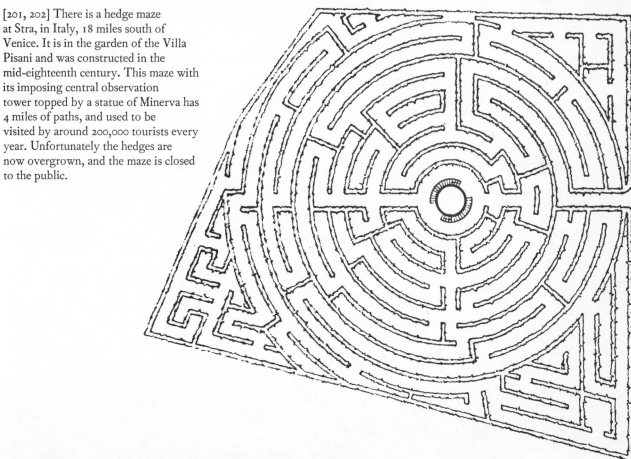

## Hedge Mazes in Britain and North America

[203 *above*] An early hedge maze in England was in the garden at Theobalds, Hertfordshire. It was constructed around 1560, but was destroyed shortly afterwards, being 'demolish'd by the rebels' (according to John Evelyn's *Memoirs*) in the early 1640s.

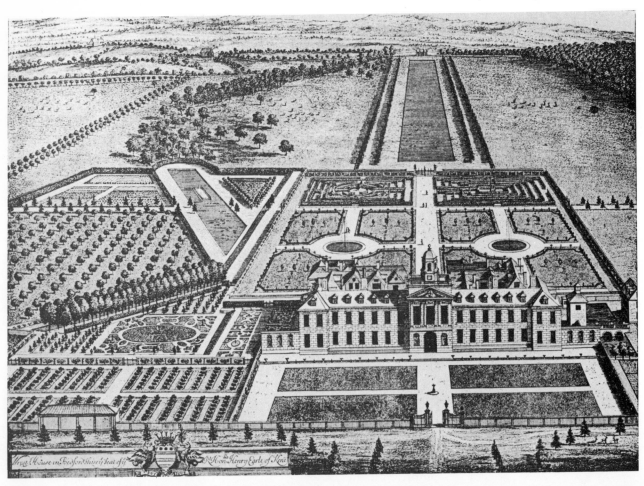

[204, 205] Very formal hedge mazes
were once to be seen in the grounds
of Wrest House, Bedfordshire (*left*) and
Badminton, Gloucestershire (*right*),
illustrated in these engravings by J. Kip
from the early eighteenth century.

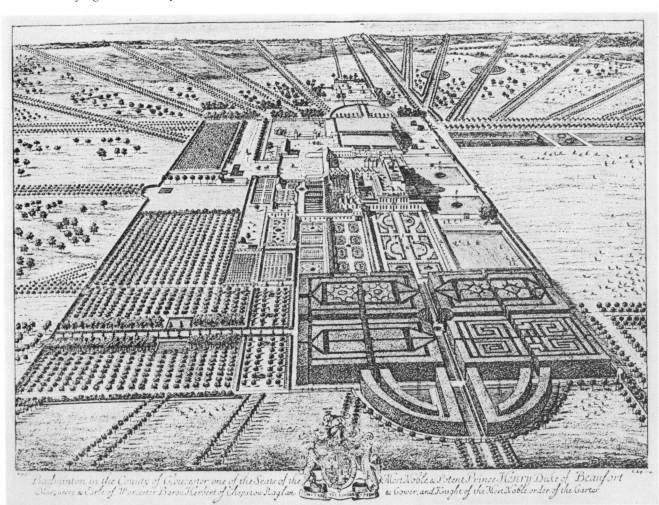

Badminton in the County of Gloucester one of the Seats of the ... Most Noble & Potent Prince Henry Duke of Beaufort
Marquesse & Earle of Worcester Baron Herbert of Chepstow Raglan ... & Gower, and Knight of the Most Noble order of the Garter

# MAZES

From the British Museum. Harl: MSS:

Somerleyton. Hall. Suffolk

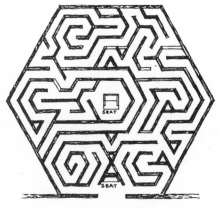

Arley Hall Cheshire

Belton House. Lincolnshire

From Thomas Hills "Arte of Gardening" 1568

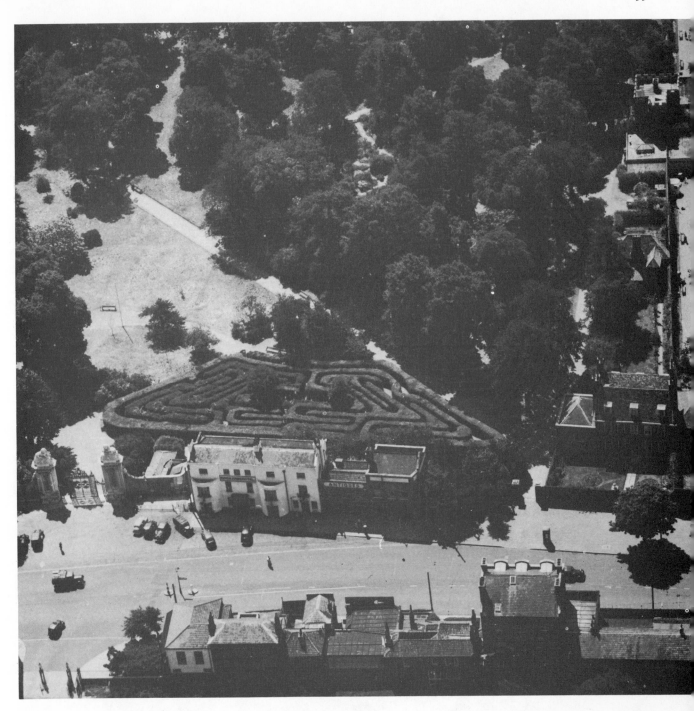

[206 *left*] This plate from *Formal Gardens in England and Scotland* by H. Inigo Triggs (1902) shows several designs of hedge and garden mazes. The example from Thomas Hill is the same as illustration 176. Of the three English examples shown, only the one at Somerleyton Hall is still in existence (see 209). The maze at Arley Hall was of hornbeam, but it was unfortunately abandoned during the Second World War and no longer exists. That at Belton House was removed in 1940, having become overgrown and straggly. It was then around 100 years old, and was formed of a 7 feet 6 inches high *Cupressus* hedge. Its diameter was approximately 120 feet.

[207] The hedge maze in the grounds of Hampton Court Palace, near London, as well as being the best-known maze in England is also the oldest surviving hedge maze in the country. It was constructed in 1690 and probably replaced an even older maze. As can be seen, it is neither large nor complex, but even so its paths extend for about half a mile.

[208 *left*] A larger maze of conventional oblong shape, with hedges of yew, occupies a prominent position in the gardens behind Hatfield House, in Hertfordshire. This example measures 174 feet by 108 feet.

[209, 210] Somerleyton Hall near Lowestoft in Suffolk possesses a fine yew hedge maze, planted in 1846 when the formal gardens surrounding the hall were laid out. The path to the 'goal' – a pagoda – is 400 yards long; illustration 206 includes a plan of the maze.

[211, 212 *left*] A maze of unusual design can be seen in the beautiful garden at Glendurgan near Falmouth, Cornwall. The hedges are of laurel, and were planted in 1833 by Alfred Fox, an ancestor of the present occupants. The following extracts are from his journal of 1833:

*23rd 4mo. Sarah and I planned a new walk to-day, through the plantation from the Cottage to the flower garden.*

*11th 5mo. Dearest Sarah, our trio, and servants left Glendurgan, after a delightful time there.*

*6th 7mo. This morning we commenced the erection of a summer-house on the side of the hill before the Cottage, with 8 sides to it . . .*

*14th 7mo. My dearest Sarah and I had an interesting discourse to-night on serious things: the road to Heaven, on scruples, faith, obedience, etc.*

*17th We rose at 4 a.m. and saw the sun eclipsed more than 4 out of 8 digits.*

*25th Sarah and I engaged with men in fitting the rustic work of our new arbour.*

*2nd 10mo. Cholera very severe at Falmouth, 48 deaths.*

*5th Began the preparation for a labyrinth at Glendurgan . . .*

*1st 11mo. I rose at 5 a.m. and went on the water till breakfast. The men still busy with the labyrinth.*

*1st 12mo. Nearly all the laurels planted to form our new labyrinth . . .*

*20th Sarah and I went to Glendurgan. Sarah closed the school for the holidays, distributing the prizes, clothes, etc. I examined the apple and pear trees planted near the labyrinth, Sarah returning with me on horseback by moonlight.*

The plan [212] of the maze was worked out by Charles Fox, son of the present manager of the Glendurgan estate.

[213] The hedge maze in the grounds of Hever Castle, Kent.

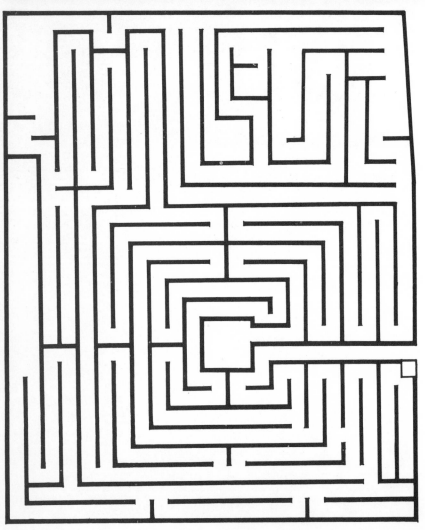

[214, 215] Hazlehead Park, Aberdeen, Scotland, has a large privet hedge maze covering three-quarters of an acre. It measures 190 feet by 160 feet approximately, and the path to the centre is 482 yards in length. Sir Henry Alexander, Lord Provost of Aberdeen from 1932 to 1935, presented the maze to the city in 1935, in gratitude for the happy times he and his family had spent at Hazlehead.

[216] This sad picture, taken in 1974, shows a decaying maze. It is in Bridge End Gardens, Saffron Walden, Essex, not far from the turf maze [80]. When Matthews described it in 1922, he wrote: '[It] is still in excellent condition, although suffering in places from the illicit short-cuts made by impatient visitors.'[51] It seems that the passage of fifty years has not improved the situation, and this example illustrates clearly that without constant attention hedge mazes soon become straggly and unsightly.

[217, 218] A quiet village in the English Cotswold Hills is the location of a small hedge maze with an unusual story. The rector of Wyck Rissington, Gloucestershire, began planting the maze in 1950 following a vivid dream in which he was given instructions by a man who stood behind him. The work took six years, and photograph 217 shows the rector with his daughters in the maze with the planting completed.

The path follows the journey of life; 'The wrong turnings are the sins and mistakes we make. The path leads through life to death, then through the garden of Paradise, to Heaven. The sign-boards connect the maze with the wonderful carvings in the Church.'[52]

St Laurence is the church's patron saint, and his day, 10 August, is celebrated every year with a special service and a procession round the maze.

Anyone who follows the path to the centre will find himself at the foot of a beautiful Wellington pine tree (*Sequoia gigantea*) planted in 1852. It was one of the first of the species planted in this country, and measures 30 feet round the trunk.

Illustration 218 shows one of the paths in 1974, nearly twenty-five years after the rector's strange dream which started his ambitious project.

[219] This fine formal hedge maze, once to be seen in the gardens surrounding Holly Croft in Dayton, Ohio, U.S.A., was, sadly, removed towards the end of the Second World War.

George B. Smith, the owner of the house before the war, and his daughter visited England where they were intrigued by the maze at Hampton Court, so Miss Smith designed a maze for their garden and it was planted in 1929. It occupied an area about 60 feet by 40 feet, and the privet hedges were around 4 feet high.

[220, 221] The maze at New Harmony, Indiana, U.S.A., had a symbolic significance for its owners, the Harmony Society. They were a German Protestant sect who went to America in 1803–4 under the leadership of their founder, George Rapp. Their first settlement in the U.S.A. was at Harmonie, Pennsylvania (now Harmony); in 1814 they formed a second settlement at Harmonie in Indiana (later named New Harmony by the Scottish socialist Robert Owen who established a Utopian colony there in 1824), and there they constructed their maze of vines and shrubs. It was described in 1822 by John Melish: 'This was a most elegant flower garden with various hedge-rows disposed in such a manner as to puzzle people to get into the little temple, emblematical of Harmony, in the middle. The Labyrinth represents the difficulty of arriving at harmony. The temple is rough on the exterior, showing that, at a distance, it has no allurements, but it is smooth and beautiful within to show the beauty of harmony when once attained.'

The following quotation explains more fully the significance the maze had for the Rappites (as they were later called): 'In connection with their practice of the universal cultivation of fine flowers, it may be assumed that the Labyrinth symbolized their belief in the early coming of the millennium. It also typified their conception of the winding ways of life by which a state of true social harmony was to be attained ultimately. It seems, furthermore, to have been regarded by them and by those who visited them, as a pleasure ground. Thus, it integrated truly the harmony of those devout people.'[53]

The maze had no meaning for the Owenites who took over Harmonie, and so it was obliterated between 1840 and 1850. The Rappites had moved to a new settlement named Economy in Pennsylvania (now Ambridge), and the society was finally dissolved in 1906. However, a New Harmony Memorial Commission was set up earlier this century, and the maze was restored in 1941 with hedges mainly of privet. The restoration used a new design, because no record of the original pattern survived.

[222] Williamsburg used to be the capital city of colonial Virginia, U.S.A., and it has since been restored to its former elegance. The 170-acre site contains many original eighteenth-century structures and 100 gardens, as well as reconstructed buildings; and in the grounds of the Governor's Palace is a hedge maze of native American holly, *Ilex opaca*. There are 1,000 feet of hedges 5–6 feet high, with four standard American hollies 20 feet tall in the centre. The maze, which is about forty years old, has external dimensions of 88 feet wide and 95 feet long.

[223] A new hedge maze is currently taking shape in Nova Scotia, Canada. Robert K. Allen, of Tree Tops, Carleton, in Yarmouth County, has planted a field with almost 1,200 young trees, mostly spruce, in the pattern shown here. Small natural spruce trees are often used for hedges in Eastern Canada, and grow abundantly in old fields and along road ditches, so the resulting maze will blend in with its surroundings. It occupies an area of 168 feet by 136 feet, and Mr and Mrs Allen intend to keep the trees clipped to a height of about 5 feet. Mr Allen was a Professional Forester with the Canadian Forestry Corps during the last war, but the Allens had the idea for their maze as a result of visiting the maze at Hampton Court. That most famous of British mazes seems to have inspired several others, including the former maze at Dayton, Ohio [219], and the holly maze at Colonial Williamsburg.

## Folk Art

[224] Most of the mazes and labyrinths illustrated so far have originated in Europe, but the same symbols can also be found in other continents. Some of the 'folk art' illustrated here is closely akin to the ancient labyrinthine designs shown earlier.

The aborigines of central Australia are a people with a history stretching back a long way into the past. Together with other 'primitive' peoples they have been looked down on, but anyone examining their art closely will realize that it has a beauty, a dignity and a depth far greater than much of the art of the Western world.

Relevant to this book are their sacred stones called 'churingas' or 'tjurungas', which often have spiral or circular designs carved on them as illustrated here. They are 'slabs of wood or stone within which the spiritual body of the "eternal uncreated" ancestor . . . [was] distributed when he touched the earth. They contained the souls of

the unborn, and their presence in the water-hole, rock or tree, which was the point of divine entry to this world, caused passing women to conceive.'[54] The strong connection between spiral designs and birth illustrated here is very reminiscent of the link between the labyrinth and rebirth described on pages 9–14.

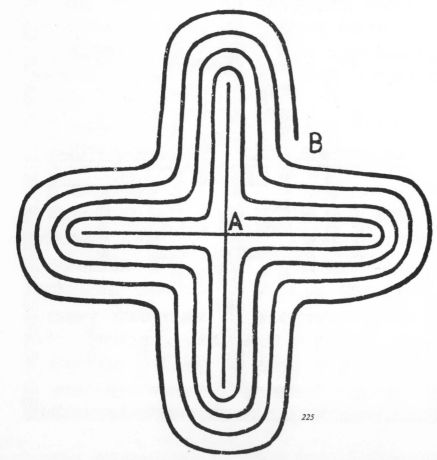

225

[225–229] About 1,000 miles north-east of Australia is the island of Malekula in the New Hebrides. Here, and on the small islands off Malekula's north-east coast, the people make intricate 'sand-tracings', and many of the traditional designs are labyrinthine in character,[55] as the illustrations show.

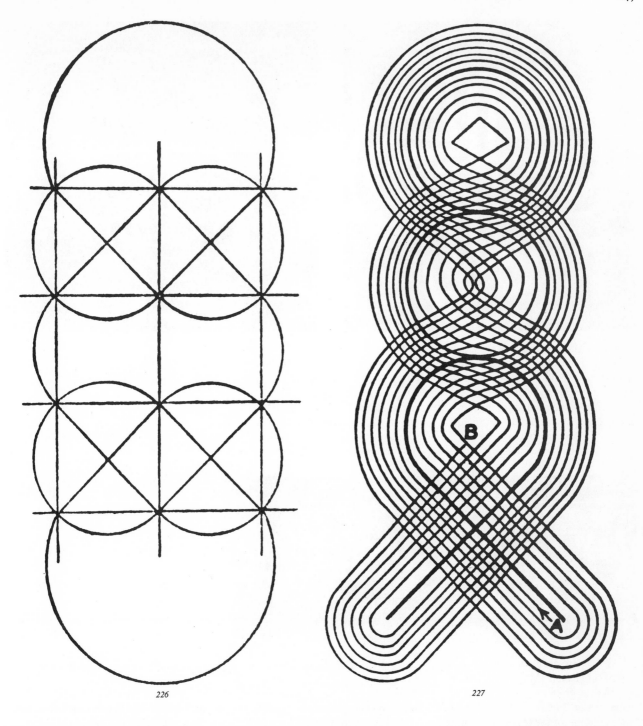

226

227

I have already mentioned in the introduction the design called 'The Path' [226] and its connection with a death ritual, and here are two more examples of the many designs collected in the same area. Illustration 225 is a sand-tracing from Vao called *na-ghimbo*, a kind of yam; 227 comes

from Oba. The sand-tracings, drawn in a continuous line without lifting the finger, are now used as games of skill, with the original significance apparently forgotten. The islanders also perform *na-leng* maze dances.

Illustrations 228 and 229 (page 146) are not sand-tracings, though they

resemble them closely. I noticed these designs when looking through *English Medieval Graffiti* by V. Pritchard,[56] and found that the author had also remarked the same similarity. They are in fact rubbings of carvings incised in a stone at the base of the tower (rebuilt in the fifteenth century) of

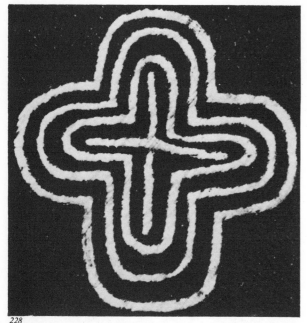

228

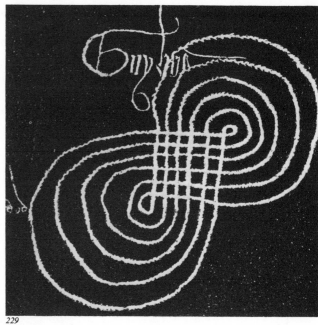

229

St Martin's church, Little Waltham, Essex. They are among a number of geometrical designs and fragments of medieval writing. 228 differs from 225 only in the number of loops separating the central cross from the outside, and in the fact that the sand-tracing design is a continuous line, whereas the graffito is not. 229 resembles 227 in the spirals and central cross-hatching. This graffito is also similar to a design on an Egyptian pre-Dynastic vase belonging to the Gerzean period (in the Fitzwilliam Museum, Cambridge). It is interesting to speculate whether these designs originated independently.

[230] Much ornate carving decorates the temple of Halebid, Mysore, in India, which dates from the twelfth and thirteenth centuries A.D., and a small section of one of the friezes illustrating an episode in the Indian epic the *Mahābhārata* includes a labyrinth. The event was supposed to have taken place in the legendary battle of Kurukshetra. 'The Pandava hero Abhimanyu had penetrated into the enemy formation and was engaged in a desperate struggle with several kawava warriors. He is shown riddled with arrows but still fighting, while the formation is symbolised by a circular labyrinth, rising up behind his back.'[57] In the *Mahābhārata*, the circular formation is described as a magical structure connected with the rites of a warrior aristocracy, and involving the active participation of a priest-magician. The main object of the labyrinth was to keep all but the chosen victim, Abhimanyu, out: he was sacrified at the centre.

This carving is not the only example of a labyrinth to be found in India. The boulder labyrinth near Kundani has already been mentioned [107], as have the threshold and tattoo designs of the south (page 11). Also in the south, labyrinths were once carved on the stone walls in front of houses among the Kota of the Nilgiri Hills. The designs were the same as those seen on the coins of Knossos [47–52], and they were called *kótē*, fort. Games were played with them, the idea of course being to reach the centre.

[231] A mandala is a ritual or magic circle used in Lamaism and Tantric yoga as a *yantra*, or aid to contemplation. They were often drawn on the ground with coloured threads or coloured rice powder, and their functional similarity to labyrinths has often been noted. Mircea Eliade explains the links between labyrinth and mandala clearly.

'The initiation of the neophyte consists, among other things, in his entering into the different zones and gaining access to the different levels of the *mandala*. This rite of penetration may be regarded as equivalent to the well-known rite of walking round a temple (*pradakshina*), or to the progressive elevation, terrace by terrace, up to the "pure lands" at the highest levels of the temple. On the other hand, the placing of the neophyte in a *mandala* may be likened to the initiation by entry into a labyrinth: certain *mandalas* have, moreover, a clearly labyrinthine character. The function of the *mandala* may be considered at least twofold, as is that of the labyrinth. On the one hand, penetration into a *mandala* drawn on the ground is equivalent to an initiation ritual; and, on the other hand, the *mandala* "protects" the neophyte against every harmful force from without, and at the same time helps him to concentrate, to find his own "centre".'[58]

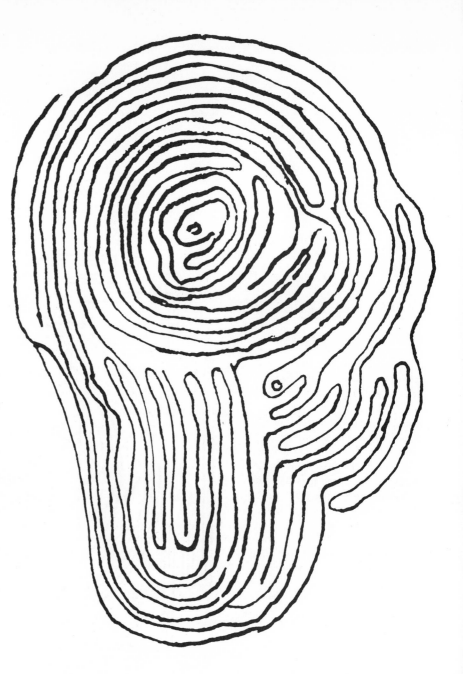

[232] Mazes and labyrinths are not
unknown on the continent of Africa.
The drawing is of a Zulu maze; they
called the goal (of which there are
two here) 'the royal hut'. In this example
the main goal is that in the top part
of the design. This drawing is taken from
L. H. Samuelson's book *Some Zulu
Customs and Folklore*,[59] where the author
describes the Zulu mazes as follows.

'The Zulus are very fond of drawing
mazes (usogexe) on the ground with
the finger, or – after smoking hemp
(insangu) – with saliva passed
through a hollow stem of tambootie
grass and so made to trace a labyrinth (tshuma sogexe) on a smooth floor.
The one who draws generally asks
some one else to find the way into the
royal hut. And this he does with a
pointer of tambootie, or failing to follow
the right course and getting cornered,
is greeted with a general shout of
"Wapuka sogexe!" (you are done
for in the labyrinth), and has to go back
to the start and begin the quest again.
This game is a great favourite, and is
often played for hours at a time: the
sons of Mpanda were great adepts at it.
They would vary it sometimes by
dotting rows of warriors on the outside,
and then success depended on the
positions that the combatants were made
to assume, the great triumph being
to bring an army with the shape of a
bull's head and horns, when he whose
horn first touched the adversary's
line was acclaimed as winner.'

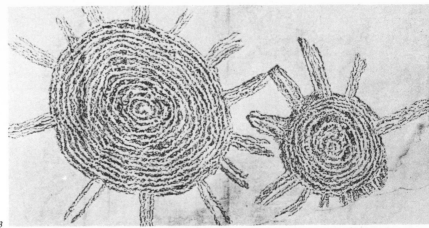

233

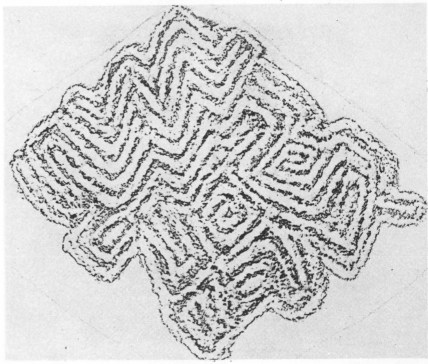

234

[233, 234] A number of rock engravings
in Griqualand West and Bechuanaland
(now Botswana), South Africa, are
enigmatic because they cannot be dated,
and no one is certain who carved them.
It is thought that the oldest are 'many
centuries old', and the two geometrical
designs shown here come into that cat-
egory. 233 was discovered at Schoolplaats
on the Vaal River, and the design is
reminiscent of the Australian aborigine
churingas illustrated earlier [224]. It
has been suggested that such designs
were the work of sun worshippers.

234, found at Klipfontein, strongly
resembles a labyrinth.

150

[235] Several square and circular spiral labyrinths decorate this copper plaque. It was made during the period A.D. 700–1000, and comes from the Aguada culture of the north-west Argentine in South America.

236

237

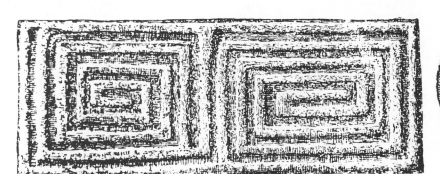

238

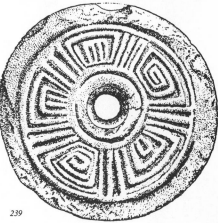

239

[236–239] Further examples of the use of maze-like designs on artefacts from the American continent are these colour stamps and spindle-whorls from Mexico and Venezuela. Circular and square spirals forming elementary labyrinths can be clearly seen.

236 and 237 are terracotta colour stamps from Tlaltelolco, Mexico. They were made from soft clay, baked hard, and were used by coating the design with colour and pressing it on to the object to be decorated.

238 is another terracotta colour stamp, used by the Piaroa Indians of Venezuela (they were still in use at the end of the last century) to decorate their bodies with designs in paint when they attended feasts and meetings, and as a protection against insects.

239 is a terracotta spindle-whorl from the Valley of Mexico.

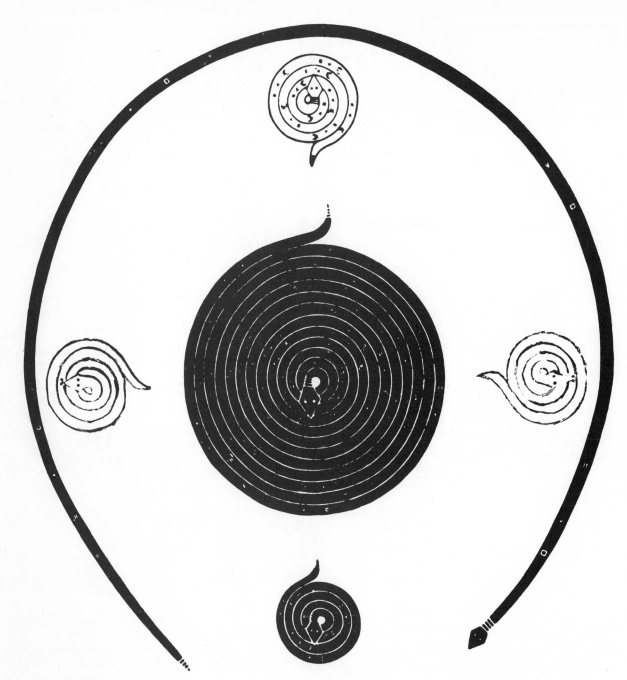

[240] The Navajo Indians of North
America make sand-paintings for the
purpose of ritual healing. The Medicine
Man 'paints' on the ground by letting
the sand flow through his fingers. He
sometimes also uses corn meal,
flower pollen, powdered roots and bark,
and ashes. Serpents are often depicted
in the spiral, labyrinthine designs, for the
Navajo credit them with special power.

[241, 242] The American Indians also use maze designs in their art and craft work. 241 is a modern Navajo double saddle blanket; 242 is a Pima Indian basketry tray. The Pima design is called *Siuhü ki* and represents the house of Siuhü who figured in several Pima legends. He lived far in the mountains where trails became so confused that no one could follow him.

[243] A carved wooden box from Kanpanger, Norway, illustrates the traditional use of the maze design in Scandinavian craftwork. In Iceland also the labyrinth or *Völundarhús* was sometimes chosen as a wood-carving design, one example still in existence being an eighteenth-century bedboard decorated with a carving of the 'labyrinth of man's life'.

154

## The 19th and 20th Centuries

[244] An oak cabinet in the William Morris room at the Victoria and Albert Museum, London, has two inlaid mazes as part of its decoration. The cabinet was designed by J. P. Seddon in 1861, and painted by Ford Madox Brown, Edward Burne Jones, Dante Gabriel Rossetti and William Morris with scenes from Sir Walter Scott's *Anna von Geierstein*.

[245] The popular Victorian children's maze puzzle 'Pigs in Clover' was featured in a political cartoon in *Punch* in the 1880s.[60] The politician is, of course, Gladstone, and his problem is again topical today.

THE SHAMROCK PUZZLE.

"I THINK I SHALL GET 'EM ALL IN,—IN TIME!"

[246] 'The Labyrinth of London' appeared in *The Strand Magazine* in April 1908,[61] and the instructions read: 'The traveller is supposed to enter by the Waterloo Road, and his object is to reach St Paul's Cathedral without passing any of the barriers which are placed across those streets supposed to be under repair.'

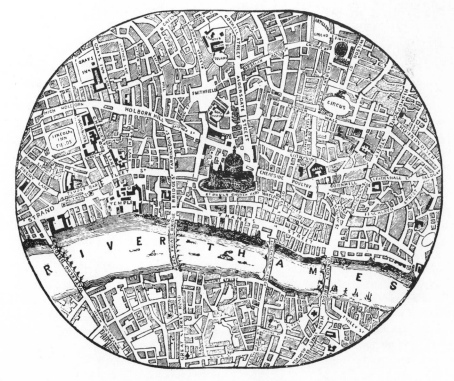

[247] The predominant colours in Friedensreich Hundertwasser's 'Der Grosse Weg' (Le Grand Chemin/La Strada/The Big Way) (1955), shown here, are blue and red. Born in 1928 in Vienna, where he lives now, Hundertwasser has produced other paintings on the same theme, among them 'Das Herz der Revolution' (1958 and 1963), 'Kaaba-Penis' (1959) and 'Sonne und Spiraloide über dem Roten Meer' (1960). All are oil on canvas.

[248] 'Irrgarten' is the title of Arnold
Leissler's maze painting (painted 1962,
oil on canvas). Leissler was born in
Hannover, West Germany, in 1939,
and now lives in Nürnberg.

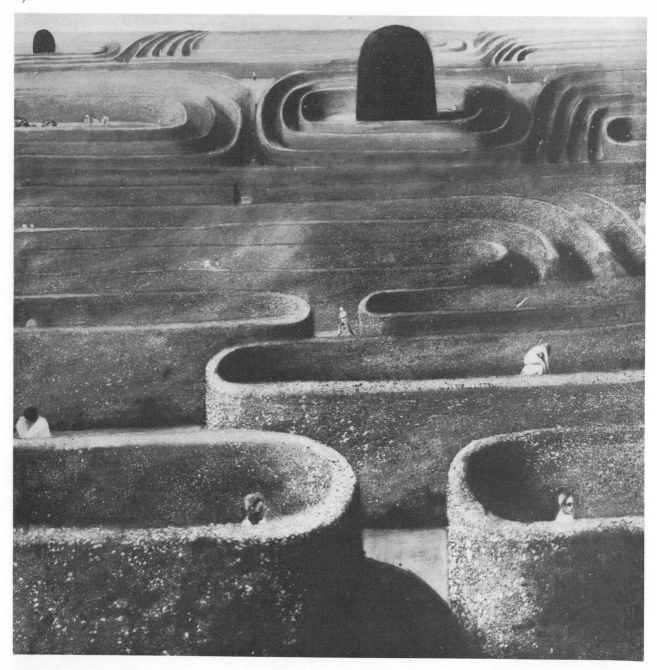

[249] 'Maze with Running Boy' (painted 1970, oil on canvas) is only one example of many paintings by Rosie Lee which incorporate the labyrinth visually or symbolically. Born in 1935 in Rotterdam of English parents, she writes: 'For me the journey in the maze is a journey in my own world or inner self . . . I'm not sure why I started painting mazes. At the time, 1969, I regarded my work as mainly therapeutic; since, it has become more philosophic.

'May I quote a few lines a friend sent me this summer: "The fresh breeze went brushing all the thick hedges which divide the gardens. Somehow, extraordinary emotions possessed me. I forget now what. Often now I have to control my excitement – as if I were pushing through a screen, or as if something beat fiercely close to me." (Virginia Woolf) She says in words what I want to paint about.'

[250 *right*] John Willenbecher's 'Labyrinth 17.IV.72' was painted in 1972, the medium being gesso, acrylic and crayon on masonite. The artist, an American, was born in 1936 and lives in New York City. The labyrinth symbol features in much of his work, constructions as well as paintings and works on paper, and early in 1975 many of his labyrinths were on display in the Everson Museum of Art in Syracuse, New York.

[251–253] A modern version of the Cretan labyrinth has been constructed by artist, sculptor and writer Michael Ayrton (born London 1921, died 1975), at Dry Brook, Arkville in the Catskill Mountains, New York State, U.S.A. The maze, of brick and stone, took two years to build. The walls are 8 feet high, and the passageways extend for 1,680 feet. There are two central chambers, each containing a large bronze – Daedalus/Icarus Matrix, and a 7-foot Minotaur. (The Minotaur is also in Postman's Park near St Paul's, London; and the Arkville maze may be seen by arrangement with the owner Mrs S. Erpf.)

Michael Ayrton had long been haunted by the legend of Daedalus, and in 1967 he wrote his 'life' in a powerful novel entitled *The Maze Maker*.[62] In it Daedalus comments: 'Each man's life is a labyrinth at the centre of which lies his death, and even after death it may be that he passes through a final maze before it is all ended for him. Within the great maze of a man's life are many smaller ones, each seemingly complete in itself, and in passing through each one he dies in part, for in each he leaves behind him a part of his life and it lies dead behind him. It is a paradox of the labyrinth that its centre appears to be the way to freedom.'

[254] The world exhibition EXPO 67 was held in Canada, and the general theme was 'Man and his World'. One of the most ambitious projects staged was 'Labyrinthe', a contemporary retelling of the story of Theseus and the Minotaur, but showing man's conquest of himself. The symbolism was explained by Director Roman Kroitor: 'The architectural structure is the world and the path followed by the audience while wending its way through the building is a thread of a person's life. The theatres are life's experiences and the "beast" is the inevitably incomplete realization of one's nature which we hoped would be conquered or dispelled as one moved through the various phases of "Labyrinthe".'

Sophisticated cinema techniques were employed to help create the effect, and the essential story of man was told in a 45-minute film prepared by the National Film Board of Canada. In the five-storey building, 720 people at a time moved through three chambers, on one occasion gazing down onto a huge screen 40 feet below.

The three chambers are described in the exhibition guidebook: 'In the first long, high chamber spectators experience a sense of participation comparable to dropping out into space, with the world left far below. In the second chamber, visitors move along walkways set between mirrored glass prisms. In the final chamber, the audience faces a multiscreen battery of unparalleled scope – using five screens, so that areas of the mind are exercised that almost certainly have not been exercised before.'

By the time EXPO 67 closed on 20 October 1967, 1,324,560 people had visited the pavilion, many of them having queued for up to seven hours.

[255] This poster, advertising the accessibility of Hampton Court maze by Green Line coach, was designed in 1956 by F. H. K. Henrion for London Transport.

A harassed school teacher from Hayes
Took her children to Hampton Court Maze,
They got thoroughly lost
At a moderate cost
And then had a wonderful time admiring
the Great Vine and imagining Henry VIII
serving double faults on the Tennis Court.
It was easy to get there, too — Green Line
Coaches 716, 716A, 718 and 725 run to the gates.

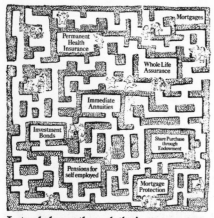

Let us help you through the insurance maze.

Finding the right insurance for your needs is a difficult, if not hazardous exercise whether you're after a tax savings plan, a life protection policy or a pension scheme.

There are so many forms of insurance (or is it assurance?) that even the jargon is confusing – immediate annuity, whole life, permanent health, unit linked life assurance.... The list seems unending.

And by the time you have spoken to a number of insurance companies, compared one set of figures with another and read all the small print, you begin to wonder if anyone understands the difference between insurance and assurance after all.

To help you sort it all out, call in a good life assurance broker before you start

your search – a broker like Glanvills.

We have spent many years specialising in the life and pensions field and are based in the heart of things in the City. Furthermore, as a member of the Charterhouse Group, a £50 million company with widespread investments, we are exceptionally well placed to know what is happening in trade and industry.

If you want maximum money growth with minimum tax liability, come and talk to us. Telephone Tim Dixon at 01-283 4622, or drop him a line at the address below.

**Glanvills**

Glanvill Enthoven (Life Pensions & Mortgages) Ltd, 144 Leadenhall Street, London EC3P 3BJ.

alfa romeo 1900

si svincola dalle spire del traffico

no puzzle !

**TIRANTI for Art books sculptorsTools**

70 High Street, Theale, Berkshire.

[256–258] Three advertisements using mazes to make their point; that insurance is a maze where you need an experienced guide; that in present-day traffic you should use a car which will get you out of jams quickly; and that there is an easy answer to the puzzle of where to buy art books!

HARP SPECIAL LAGER

[259] Another version of the labyrinth used in an advertisement, this time as a beermat advertising Harp Special Lager.

# A. HOUTSCHILD

**International Scientific Bookseller
13 Papestraat
THE HAGUE, HOLLAND**

[260] A bookseller promoting English books in the Netherlands has chosen a labyrinth as his trademark. He comments on his choice: 'A labyrinth has something mystical or mysterious – a hard way to a target. That is my personality, perhaps my career (I was a military cryptanalyser – secret codes, etc.). Apart from this my bookshop specializes in art and history and architecture. The labyrinth is from the cathedral of Rheims, so here is the link between the trademark and the books we carry.'

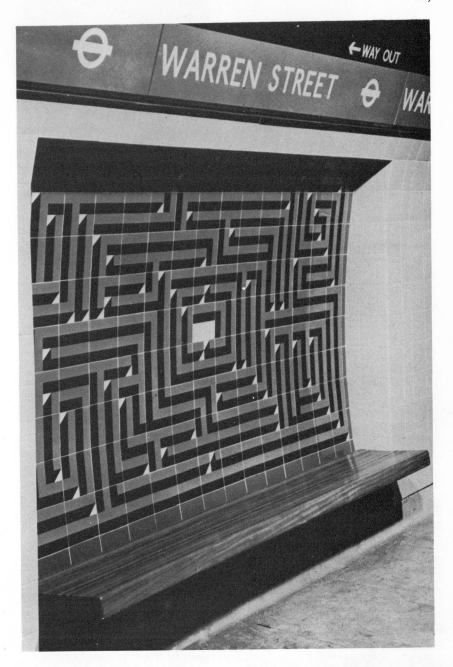

[261] Warren Street 'warren' is a striking
design which can be seen behind each
bench on the Victoria Line platforms at
London's Warren Street underground
station. The motif is described as 'a visual
pun representing a maze', and was
designed by Crosby/Fletcher/Forbes.
The station was opened for passengers
on 1 December 1968.

[262] Mirror mazes are popular in fairs and at the seaside. This is the entrance to the maze at the end of Southend pier, Essex.

[263 *below*] On Good Friday, 1971, Greg Bright (author of *Greg Bright's Maze Book*) began to dig this maze at Pilton, Somerset. It took him about a year, and in that time he dug over a mile of trenches ranging from 18 inches to 6 feet deep.

He also undertakes commissions to design mazes for other people, and the new yew hedge maze designed by him for Longleat House, Wiltshire, incorporates bridges and underpasses.

[264] A topical cartoon in 1974 from the magazine *Reveille*. 'That's his "hedge against inflation". The postman can't get at the letter-box with any bills.'

[265] Labyrinth themes are often found in literature, sometimes in retellings of Theseus's story, sometimes in original creations. The plan shown here is from *The Tombs of Atuan* by Ursula Le Guin,[63] a 'strange, original and stirring story' written ostensibly for children but which adults too will find gripping.

[266] A maze set out at a free festival at Oxford on May Day 1974 proved very popular – with adults, children, and dogs!

[267, 268] These are examples of the work of two former students at Kingston upon Thames Polytechnic, Surrey, John Barnatt and Ken Beagley. Their studies culminated in an exhibition of their Fine Art Diploma work, entitled 'Mazes', which was held in Kingston Museum and Art Gallery during the summer of 1974. The principle behind the 'light-bulb maze' is that you can move from one square to another only when a light goes out.

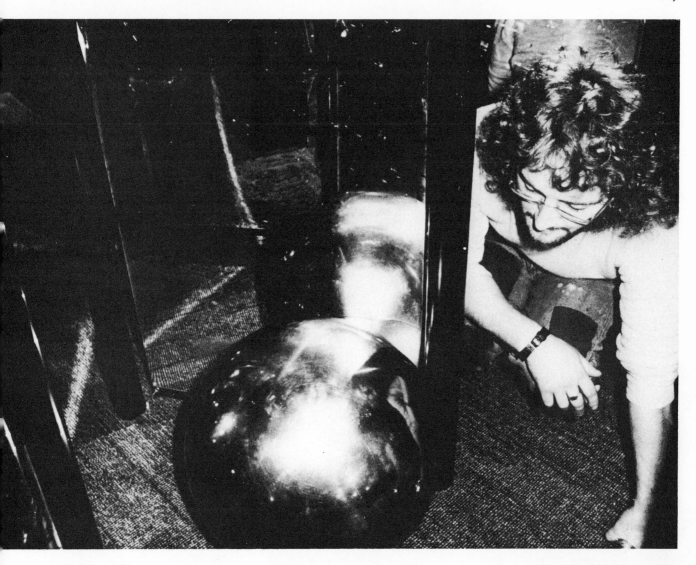

[269] 'Labyrinth' was a two-storey maze exhibited at the Midland Group Gallery for four weeks during the Nottingham Festival in July 1971. Five artists from the Midlands were involved – Ralph Selby (whose idea it was), Peter Smailes, Geoff Heaton, Chris Dawson and Stroud Cornock.

On the ground floor an arrangement of silver Melinex panels supported by plastic drainpipes formed an ingenious maze in a very small space 17 feet by 34 feet. Wanderers might suddenly be confronted by one of five large steel spheres moving through the maze under their own power (see photograph). The 'goal' of the maze was a machine which, if a suitable message was spoken to it, delivered a badge.

Upstairs was a second maze of similar construction, but in total darkness. Those bold enough to enter it were given a survival kit ('suss-pack') of a torch (which went on and off at random) and headphones (which occasionally picked up localized sounds such as the dawn chorus, the National Anthem, or readings from *Alice in Wonderland*. The 'sound messages' were periodically switched from one locality to another, and so both torch and headphones supplied information which provided an unreliable guide to the wanderer.

'Labyrinth' was extremely successful, attracting around 7,000 visitors. Ralph Selby comments: 'We were soon overwhelmed by a continuous queue, so that we had to institute an appointments book, hire a receptionist and train two guides. Each of the two levels was only sixty square yards, but even in this small space the people of Nottingham showed a great capacity to get lost. . . . It seemed that no visitor was in doubt as to what the Labyrinth was about and it seemed to be enjoyed for much the same reasons as the five of us built it. I was surprised by the way a usually cynical public was prepared to suspend their disbelief – and of course it was the most confident who found themselves more quickly trapped than the cautious. Most visitors reported that moment of heightened awareness of their own reactions when they realised they couldn't find an immediate exit.'[64]

# Notes

Where bibliographical details
are not given in full,
the missing information can be found
in the bibliography.

1. For a full explanation of this theory, see 'The Labyrinth' by L. J. D. Richardson in *Proceedings of the Cambridge Colloquium on Mycenaean Studies* edited by L. R. Palmer and John Chadwick.

2. *The Palace of Minos at Knossos*, Macmillan, London, 1921–36; Agathon Press, New York, 1963.

3. *The Greek Myths*, vol. 1, Penguin Books, Harmondsworth, 1955.

4. The method is given fully in Richardson, op. cit.

5. For more information on this, see *Before Civilization* (The Radiocarbon Revolution and Prehistoric Europe) by Colin Renfrew, Jonathan Cape, London, 1973.

6. 'Geometrical Drawings from Malekula and Other Islands of the New Hebrides'.

7. In *Labyrinth Studien* (Labyrinthos, als Linienreflex einer mythologische Idee), Zurich, 1950.

8. 'Myth and Legend at Troy'.

9. Pitman Publishing, London, 1970.

10. Colin Still, *Shakespeare's Mystery Play, A Study of the Tempest*, London, 1922.

11. 'Labyrinth Ritual in South India – Threshold and Tattoo Designs'.

12. In *Cumaean Gates*.

13. 'The Secret of the Grail' by Geoffrey Russell in *Glastonbury, A Study in Patterns*, Research into Lost Knowledge Organisation, London, 1969.

14. Peter Fleming, *One's Company*, London, 1934.

15. *Cumaean Gates*.

16. From 'Kore' by Karl Kerényi, in *Introduction to a Science of Mythology* by C. G. Jung and K. Kerényi, Routledge & Kegan Paul, London, 1951.

17. *Cumaean Gates*.

18. Norman O. Brown, *Love's Body*, Vintage Book, New York, 1966.

19. Brown, op. cit., with quotes from G. R. Levy, *The Gate of Horn*, and Sigmund Freud, *New Introductory Lectures*.

20. *Cumaean Gates*.

21. By a Dr Böhl, in a paper read to the Societas Classica in Leiden, 1931.

22. In his article 'The Secret of the Grail', see note 13.

23. Lactantius, *De Mort. Persec.*, c. 44.

24. *Cumaean Gates*.

25. 'Notices of Ancient and Medieval Labyrinths'.

26. The Viking Press, New York, 1963.

27. *Cumaean Gates*.

28. The full interpretation appears in vol. 4, *The Dying God*, but not in the abridged version.

29. Mrs Bury Palliser, *Historic Devices, Badges, and War-Cries*, Sampson Low, Son & Marston, London, 1870.

30. *Mazes and Labyrinths*.

31. *Natural History*, XXXVI, 13, 19.

32. *Cumaean Gates*.

33. Faber paperback, London, 1961.

34. Maria-Gabriele Wosien, *Sacred Dance* (Encounter with the Gods), Thames and Hudson, London, 1974.

35. M. A. Courtney, *Cornish Feasts and Folk-lore*, first published 1890, republished by E.P. Publishing, East Ardsley, 1973.

36. W. C. Wade, *W. Antiquary*, April 1881.

37. *The Golden Bough*, vol. 4, *The Dying God*.

38. Several are illustrated in 'Troy Town' by R. Morton Nance.

39. For those who are interested, more details of Frederick Hirsch's research can be found in his *Erziehungkunst Monatschrift zur Pädagogik*, Stuttgart, 1962.

40. Roger Caillois, *Man, Play and Games*, Thames and Hudson, London, 1962.

41. *Cumaean Gates*.

42. More details are given in *An Account of the Primitive Tribes and Monuments of the Nilagiris*, by J. W. Breeks, India Museum, London, 1873.

43. *The Mystic Spiral*.

44. 'The Iconography of Dürer's "Knots" and Leonardo's "Concatenations"' in *Art Quarterly*, vol. VII, no. 2, Spring 1944.

45. Prentice Hall International, 1961.

46. 'Chartres Maze: a model of the universe?' by Critchlow, Carroll and Lee.

47. Wosien, op. cit.

48. Joseph L. Henderson & Maud Oakes, *The Wisdom of the Serpent* (The Myths of Death, Rebirth and Resurrection), George Braziller, New York, 1963.

49. In 'The Labyrinth Man', *The Connoisseur*, vol. LXXVIII, 1927, p. 232.

50. 'An Emblematic Portrait by Dosso', *Journal of the Warburg and Courtauld Institutes*, vol. 29, 1966, p. 433; reprinted in *Dosso and Battista Dossi, Court Painters at Ferrara*, Princeton University Press, Princeton, 1968.

51. *Mazes and Labyrinths*.

52. From 'Guide to Church & Maze', Wyck Rissington.

53. Both quotations are taken from *The Labyrinth* by Ross F. Lockridge, New Harmony Memorial Commission, 1941.

54. From *The Gate of Horn* by G. Rachel Levy, Faber & Faber, London, 1948 (also published as *Religious Conceptions of the Stone Age* by Harper Torchbooks, New York, 1963).

55. A full description is given in Chapter XXV, 'Sand Tracings from Vao and Atchin', in *Stone Men of Malekula* by John Layard, Chatto and Windus, London, 1942.

56. Cambridge University Press, Cambridge, 1967.

57. S. C. Brooks, 'The Labyrinth Pattern in India'.

58. *Images and Symbols*, Harvill Press, London, 1961.

59. The Church Printing Co., London, 1928.

60. 16 November 1889.

61. Vol. 35, no. 208, p. 446.

62. Longmans, Green, London, 1967.

63. Published by Victor Gollancz, London, 1972, and in paperback by Puffin Books, Harmondsworth, 1974.

64. 'Getting Lost', *Art and Artists*, vol. 6, no. 6, October 1971.

# Bibliography

*General Books*

Ayrton, Michael, *A Meaning to the Maze* (Seventh Jackson Knight Memorial Lecture), The Abbey Press, Abingdon-on-Thames, 1974

Deedes, C. N., 'The Labyrinth', in S. H. Hooke (ed.), *The Labyrinth* (Further Studies in the Relation Between Myth and Ritual in the Ancient World), S.P.C.K., London, 1935

Grant, Michael and Hazel, John, *Who's Who in Classical Mythology*, Weidenfeld and Nicolson, London, 1973

Knight, W. F. Jackson, *Cumaean Gates* (A Reference of the Sixth Aeneid to the Initiation Pattern), Basil Blackwell, Oxford, 1936; reissued in *Vergil: Epic and Anthropology*, ed. J. D. Christie, George Allen & Unwin, London, 1967 (published in U.S.A. by Barnes & Noble)

Matthews, W. H., *Mazes and Labyrinths* (Their History and Development), Longmans, Green, London, 1922; Dover Publications paperback edition, New York, 1970

Purce, Jill, *The Mystic Spiral* (Journey of the Soul), Thames and Hudson, London, 1974

Richardson, L. J. D., 'The Labyrinth', in L. R. Palmer and John Chadwick (eds), *Proceedings of the Cambridge Colloquium on Mycenaean Studies*, Cambridge University Press, Cambridge, 1966

Robertson, Seonaid M., *Rosegarden and Labyrinth* (A Study in Art Education), Routledge & Kegan Paul, London, 1963

Rykwert, Joseph, *The Idea of a Town*, 'Lectura Architectonica', Hilversum, 1963

Santarcangeli, Paolo, *Il Libro dei Labirinti* (Storia di un Mito e di un Simbolo), Vallecchi Editore, Firenza, 1967

*Labyrinthe*, Catalogue of an exhibition held by the Deutschen Gesellschaft für Bildende Kunst (Kunstverein Berlin) and the Akademie der Künste in Berlin, October–November 1966

*The Situationist Times*, no. 4, Paris, 1963

*Puzzle Books*

Ball, W. W. Rouse, *Mathematical Recreations and Essays*, Macmillan, London, 1892 (11th ed. 1939)

Bright, Greg, *Greg Bright's Maze Book*, Latimer New Dimensions, London, 1973

— *Greg Bright's Fontana Mazes*, Fontana, London, 1975

Dudeney, Henry Ernest, *Amusements in Mathematics*, Thomas Nelson and Sons, London, 1917; Dover Publications paperback, New York, 1959

Gardner, Martin, *More Mathematical Puzzles and Diversions*, Penguin paperback, Harmondsworth, 1966

Koziakin, Vladimir, *Mazes*, Pan paperback, London, 1972

Shepherd, Walter, *Mazes and Labyrinths* (A Book of Puzzles), Dover Publications paperback, New York, 1961 (revised version of *For Amazement Only*, Penguin paperback, Harmondsworth, 1942)

*Articles*

Banks, M. M., 'Tangled Thread Mazes', in *Folk-Lore*, vol. 46 (1935), p. 78.

Boyes, John H., 'Saffron Walden Maze', in *Essex Journal*, vol. 8, no. 3 (Autumn 1973), p. 88

Brooke, S. C., 'The Labyrinth Pattern in India', in *Folk-Lore*, vol. 63–4 (1952–3), p. 463

Colton, Harold Sellers, 'Is the House of Tcuhu the Minoan Labyrinth?', in *Science*, 29 June 1917, p. 667

— 'Troy Town on the Hopi Mesas', in *The Scientific Monthly*, vol. LVIII (February 1944), p. 129

Critchlow, Keith, Carroll, Jane, and Lee, Llewylyn Vaughn, 'Chartres Maze: A Model of the Universe?' in *Architectural Association Quarterly*, vol. 5, no. 2 (Summer 1973), p. 11

Deacon, A. Bernard, 'Geometrical Drawings from Malekula and Other Islands of the New Hebrides', in *Journal of the Royal Anthropological Institute*, vol. LXIV, pt. 1 (1934)

Gibson, Ackroyd, 'Rock-Carvings which Link Tintagel with Knossos: Bronze-Age Mazes Discovered in North Cornwall', in *Illustrated London News*, 9 January 1954, p. 46

Grigson, Geoffrey, 'Mazes in the Wanton Green', in *Country Life*, 13 September 1962

Hildburgh, W. L., 'The Places of Confusion and Indeterminability in Mazes and Maze-Dances', in *Folk-Lore*, vol. 56 (1945), p. 188

Knight, W. F. Jackson, 'Maze Symbolism and the Trojan Game', in *Antiquity*, vol. VI, no. 24 (December 1932), p. 445

— 'Myth and Legend at Troy', in *Folk-Lore*, vol. 46 (1935), p. 98

Layard, John, 'The Labyrinth in the Megalithic Areas of Malekula . . .', in *Man*, January 1935, 13, article no. 10

— 'Maze-Dances and the Ritual of the Labyrinth in Malekula', in *Folk-Lore*, vol. 47 (1936), p. 123

— 'Labyrinth Ritual in South India – Threshold and Tattoo Designs', in *Folk-Lore*, vol. 48 (1937)

McDonnell, John, 'The Significance of Turf Mazes', in *Country Life Annual* (1959), p. 109

Nance, R. Morton, 'Troy Town', in *Journal of the Royal Institution of Cornwall*, no. 71 (1924)

Ore, Oystein, 'An Excursion into Labyrinths', in *The Mathematics Teacher*, May 1959, p. 367

Robinson, David N., 'Julian's Bower', in *Lincolnshire Life*, vol. 9, no. 3 (May 1969), p. 28

Trollope, Edward, 'Notices of Ancient and Medieval Labyrinths', in *The Archaeological Journal*, vol. VX (1858)

Verbrugge, A.-R., 'Un Curieux Bas-Relief à Compiègne', in *Oise Tourisme*, Autumn 1970, p. 17

# Acknowledgements

My research has been greatly assisted by the work of my predecessors, and I am especially indebted to two books: *Mazes and Labyrinths* by W. H. Matthews, and *Cumaean Gates* by W. F. Jackson Knight, both of which should be read in conjunction with this book.

I would also like to express my thanks to the many people who have taken an interest in this book's preparation, and especially to those who have provided information and illustrations. I am very appreciative of the help given to me by my publisher John L. Smith, and the enthusiasm he and Sandy Carr have shown. A mention is also due to the staff of Westminster City Libraries, Maida Vale branch, who always cope so efficiently with my many requests for books. A behind-the-scenes worker who deserves special thanks is my husband Colin, who has not only done much photographic work but also provided me with very necessary encouragement.

I am grateful to the following bodies and individuals for giving permission for their copyright material to be used. Every effort has been made to trace copyright holders, and if any errors or omissions are brought to the publisher's notice, they will be corrected or included in the next edition.

## Text Acknowledgements

Agathon Press, Inc., for an extract from *The Palace of Minos at Knossos* by Sir Arthur Evans; George Allen & Unwin Ltd, Barnes & Noble, Inc., and Professor G. R. Wilson Knight for extracts from *Vergil: Epic and Anthropology* edited by J. D. Christie; The Architectural Association, for an extract from 'Chartres Maze: a model of the universe?' by Keith Critchlow, Jane Carroll and Llewylyn Vaughn Lee (This article first appeared in the *Architectural Association Quarterly*, London, Volume 5, No. 2, Summer 1973, and is reproduced by permission of the Editor.); George Braziller,

Inc., for an extract from *The Wisdom of the Serpent* by Joseph L. Henderson and Maud Oakes, reprinted with the permission of the publisher (Copyright © 1963 by Joseph L. Henderson and Maud Oakes); Ian Christie, for an extract from 'Getting Lost' in *Art and Artists*, vol. 6, no. 6, October 1971; The Estate of Sir James Frazer, for an extract from *The Golden Bough* by J. G. Frazer; Harvill Press Ltd, for an extract from *Images and Symbols* by Mircea Eliade; Penguin Books Ltd and Nicholas Thompson Ltd, for an extract from *The Maze Maker* by Michael Ayrton (reprinted by permission. of Penguin Books Ltd, copyright © Michael Ayrton, 1967); Routledge & Kegan Paul Ltd, for an extract from *Introduction to a Science of Mythology* by C. J. Jung and K. Kerényi; Thames and Hudson Ltd, for extracts from *The Mystic Spiral* by Jill Purce and *Sacred Dance* by Maria-Gabriele Wosien; The Editors of the *Journal* of the Warburg and Courtauld Institutes and Professor Felton L. Gibbons for an extract from 'An Emblematic Portrait by Dosso' by Felton Gibbons in the *Journal*, vol. XXIX, 1966.

## Illustration Acknowledgements

(Numbers refer to the illustration numbers)

Aerofilms Ltd, 207, 208, 213
Alfa Romeo, 257
Soprintendenza alle Antichità della Lombardia, 118, 120
Antikvariskt-Topografiska Arkivet, Stockholm, 99, 102, 106
Michael Ayrton, 251, 252, 253
Peter Baker Photography, 13
Bayerische Staatsbibliothek, Munich (Clm 14731, fol. 82v & 83r), 123, 124
Ken Beagley, 76, 84, 95, 266
Biblioteca Apostolica Vaticana, 126
Bibliothèque Nationale, Paris, 121, 140
Basil Blackwell and John Lloyd (8, 18, 38 from *Cumaean Gates* by W. F. Jackson Knight)

Janet and Colin Bord, 3, 4, 34, 69, 78, 79, 80, 82, 83, 157, 158, 159, 161, 162, 163, 164, 165, 166, 209, 210, 211, 218, 244, 267, 268
Trustees of the British Museum, 11, 47, 48, 49, 50, 51, 52, 53, 56, 63, 65
British Tourist Authority, 91, 92
Caisse Nationale des Monuments Historiques, Paris, 141, 143, 144
Cambridge University Press (32 from 'The Labyrinth' by L. J. D. Richardson in *Proceedings of the Cambridge Colloquium on Mycenaean Studies*, edited by L. R. Palmer and John Chadwick; 228, 229 from *English Medieval Graffiti* by V. Pritchard)
Jonathan Cape Ltd and Alfred A. Knopf, Inc. (25, 26, 27, 28 from *Camonica Valley* by Emmanuel Anati)
Archives du Centre de Recherches Archéologiques du Vexin Français, 151
Chatto and Windus Ltd and the Author's Literary Estate (225, 226, 227 from *Stone Men of Malekula* by John Layard)
Paul Clough, 262
Colonial Williamsburg Photograph, 222
Commissioners of Public Works in Ireland, 19, 20
Corporation of the City of Aberdeen, 214
Crown copyright, reproduced with permission of the controller of Her Majesty's Stationery Office, 12, 17
Deighton, Bell & Co. (233, 234 from *The Rock-Engravings of Griqualand West and Bechuanaland South Africa* by M. Wilman)
Department of Egyptology, University College London (40, 41 from *The Labyrinth Gerzeh and Mazghuneh* by W. M. Flinders Petrie; 42, 43, 44 from *Button and Design Scarabs* by W. M. Flinders Petrie)
Design Objectives Ltd, 96
Stig Englund RAGU, 100, 101
Mary Evans Picture Library, 200, 246
Fitzwilliam Museum, Cambridge, 171
Fox Photos Ltd, 217
Frick Art Reference Library, 167, 168, 169

# Index

The numbers refer to picture numbers except for those in *italic* which refer to the pages of the introductory text 'Mazes and Labyrinths'.

Dutton Paperbacks of Related Interest